AF378169

JAPANESE HAIKU for Cat Lovers

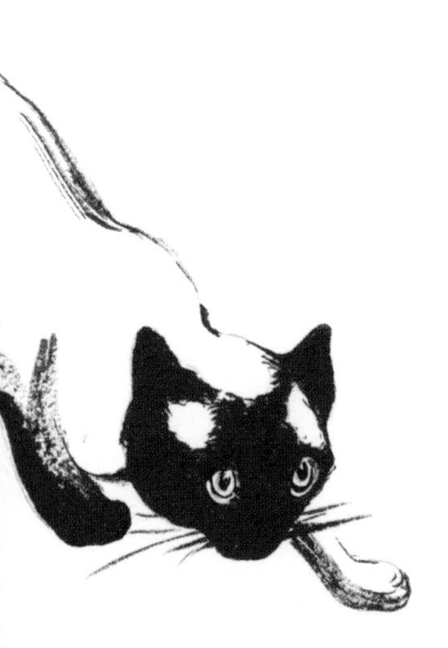

JAPANESE HAIKU for Cat Lovers

Compiled and illustrated by
Manda

Translated and introduced by
William Scott Wilson

TUTTLE Publishing

Tokyo | Rutland, Vermont | Singapore

To Access Audio Recordings for the Poems:

1. Check to be sure you have an Internet connection.
2. Type the URL below into your web browser.

www.tuttlepublishing.com/japanese-haiku-for-cat-lovers

For support, you can email us at info@tuttlepublishing.com.

The Japanese Cat

深草に猫とびうちの尻尾かな
Fukakusa ni neko tobiuchi no shippo kana

In the deep grass
the cat pounces
on its tail.

—ANONYMOUS

眼前是什麻
Ganzen kore nan zo

What is this right before your eyes?

—ZEN SAYING

The modern domestic cat (*Felis catus*) is believed to have first arrived on Japanese shores at some time during the sixth century in the company of Buddhist monks who kept them so that they could protect the sutras and other holy texts from any damage that might be inflicted by mice. The monks would have come from China or Korea on the Asian mainland, but the cats would have had a more distant lineage, with their forebears having originated in Egypt, then spreading to

India and China as they accompanied merchants, warriors, itinerant doctors and other travelers along the Silk Road. They must have been resilient animals that were very much prized by those who kept them.

Once they had been introduced to Japan, cats became highly valued and were considered rare treasures, and by the tenth and eleventh centuries it was not unusual for them to be exchanged among the upper classes as prestigious gifts. One cat, which was offered as a gift to the emperor Ichijo, was even given a rank in the imperial court, Myobu no Otodo, meaning Chief Lady-in-Waiting of the Inner Palace. Another emperor, Uda (887–897 CE), also received a cat as a gift, and was so impressed by the creature that he was inspired to write the following entry into his diary:

> On the sixth day of the second month of the first year of the Kampo era. Taking a moment of my free time, I wish to express my joy of the cat. It arrived by boat as a gift to the late emperor, received from the hands of Minamoto no Kuwashi.
>
> The color of the fur is peerless. No one could find the words to describe it, although someone said it was reminiscent of the deepest ink. It has an air about

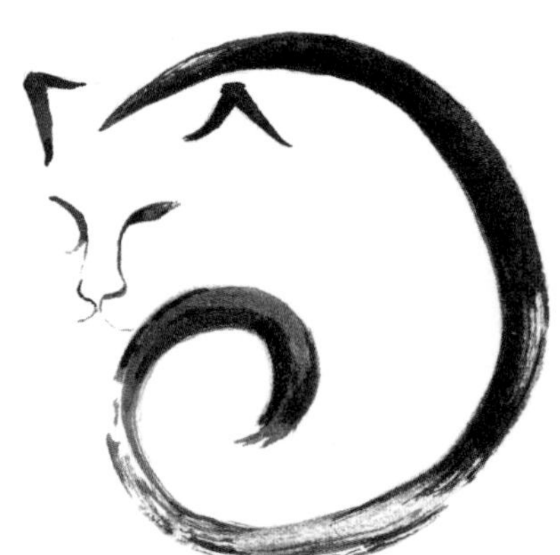

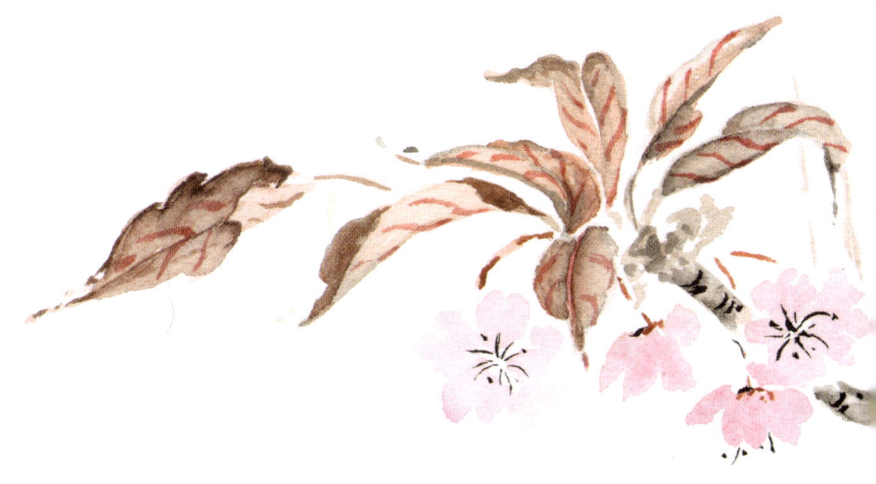

it that evokes *kanno* [the Buddhist and Taoist ideal of receptiveness and responsiveness]. Its length is 5 *sun* [1 sun is just over 1 inch or 3cm], and its height is above 6 sun. I affixed a bow about its neck, but it did not remain there for long.

In rebellion, it narrows its eyes and extends its needles. It shows its back.

When it lies down, it curls in a circle like a coin. You cannot see its feet. It's as if it were one of those Chinese jade disks with a hole in the center. When it stands, its cry expresses profound loneliness, like a black dragon above the clouds.

By nature, it likes to stalk birds. It lowers its head and works its tail. It can extend its spine to raise its height by at least 2 sun. Its color allows it to disappear at night. I am convinced it is superior to all other cats.

Emperor Uda's enthusiasm and perhaps his tinge of concern would be reflected within the general population in the years to come.

In modern Japan, cats are of course are very popular as household pets. They have an independent nature, require little care, and can be kept and maintained in small apartments in the big cities, as well as in rural areas. According to 2023 statistics, there are over nine million pet cats in Japan. There are also at least a dozen "cat islands" where feral cats outnumber the human inhabitants.

Cats are also often thought to attract good luck, prosperity and protection from unfortunate events; and black cats are even believed by some to attract desirable suitors to unmarried women. Consider the ubiquitous *maneki neko*, the little porcelain cat beckoning good fortune with its upraised paw, which can be found on the counter of almost every shop in Japan. According to a legend about the Gotokuji Temple in Tokyo, some time in the seventeenth century, when the temple was run down and in bad repair, it was inhabited only by a penniless monk and his cat. One day, a feudal lord took refuge under a large tree in the temple grounds during a heavy storm. As he rested under the tree, he noticed the cat beckoning him from the entrance to the temple. Thinking that this was strange, he left the cover of the tree,

approached the cat, and at that very moment a bolt of lightning struck the tree, causing it to fall. The man's life had been saved by the cat. As a reward, the lord bought the temple and had it rebuilt anew. When the cat died, he erected a statue of his rescuer within the temple compound which can still be seen to this day, and the little porcelain maneki neko ornaments can be bought at the temple gift store.

The popularity of Hello Kitty hardly needs to be mentioned.

There is, however, another side to this coin. Over the centuries, as the cat population began to grow and perhaps become a bit disconcerting, myths grew up about the darker sides of cats. The well-known *bakeneko*—ghost or monster cat— is thought to live way beyond normal years, to grow unusually large, and to be able to shape-shift into a human being who sometimes kills and eats other human beings. One of the signs of a bakeneko is an extraordinarily long tail, which has led some people to bob their cats' tails as a preventative measure. Related to this monster is the *nekomata*, a cat with two tails and the proclivities of its cousin. Add to these myths that around 1781, rumors began to circulate that some of the courtesans in the pleasure districts in the capital were in fact bakeneko. Ironically, such stories may have actually brought better luck to anxious wives. Or have been started by them?

Nevertheless, these tales seem not to have dampened the popularity of cats in Japan, and for those who do not have the good fortune of having their own cat as a pet, they can always pay a visit to a cat café, of which there are over sixty in Tokyo alone.

Why Cat Haiku?

Given the ubiquity and popularity of cats in Japan, it is not odd that they should appear and even "star" in popular literature. Perhaps the most well-known novel concerning a cat is *I Am a Cat* by Natsume Soseki (1867–1916), an account of human nature by an observing feline, and there are many, many more. But, why haiku?

Haiku is well known for sharing the qualities of Zen Buddhism, and cats can also be seen as having their paws in the same dish.

The supposition mentioned earlier that cats were brought to Japan only to protect religious texts from mice is perhaps a simplification. Cats were and are considered by Buddhist monks to be mindful, quick to respond, calm and concentrated—all necessary qualities for walking the Path of Zen.

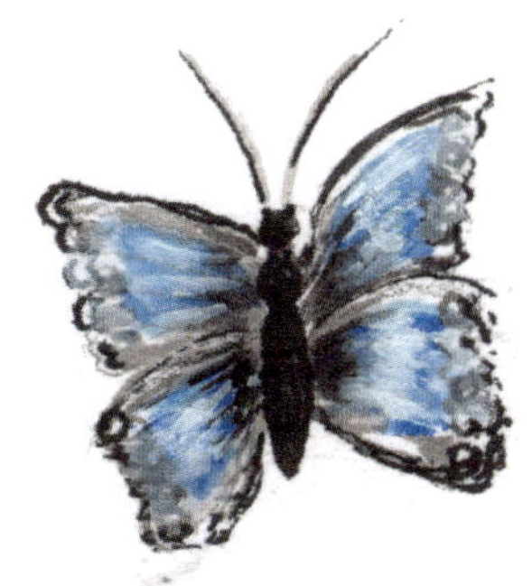

These same qualities apply to haiku. The poet must be calm and attentive enough to observe the moment, and then to express that moment without the baggage of fabrication. This is not to say that every haiku must express something of an "enlightenment" experience; some are clearly written for the poet's amusement or even as an exercise. But the prehensive requirements are the same, and cats seem to be almost gifted with these qualities by nature.

Many of the haiku in this collection were written by Kobayashi Issa (763–1828), the son of a farmer in central Japan. When his mother passed away at a young age, he often wandered alone through the fields and forests, observing the wildlife and consoling his loneliness in their company. In later life, he was a lay priest of the Jo-doshin-shu sect of Buddhism, which emphasizes a deep compassion for the marginalized and for all living beings. Issa wrote about 85 haiku about the cats he no doubt encountered on the farm and in nearby villages, and he also penned some 200 on frogs, 100 on fleas and 230 on fireflies. Although not about cats, the following haiku show the difference between Issa's outlook on the world, and that of poets like Basho, a student of Zen Buddhism, which emphasizes clarity and direct mindfulness.

An old pond,
a frog jumps in;
the sound of water.

BASHO

For you fleas, too,
the night must be long
and cold.

ISSA

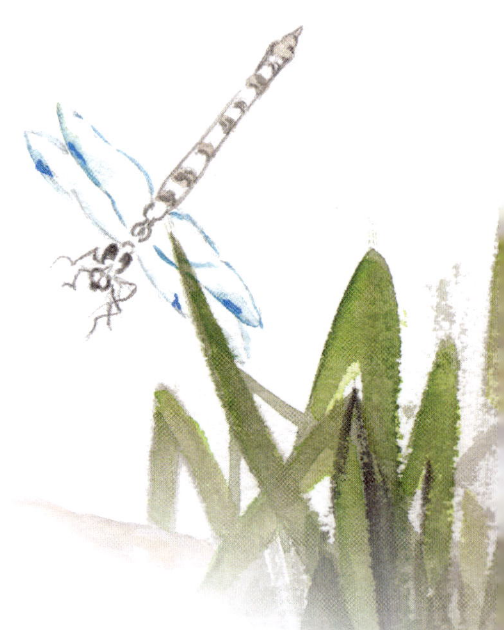

For Basho, it is the moment captured in time. For Issa, it is the life familiar to all living creatures, including cats.

If you are lucky enough to have a cat as a pet, try to observe it when you have the chance, with a quiet and empty mind. Then, as it leaps through the grass at its hidden tail, write a verse that the poets in this book might have understood intuitively.

— William Scott Wilson

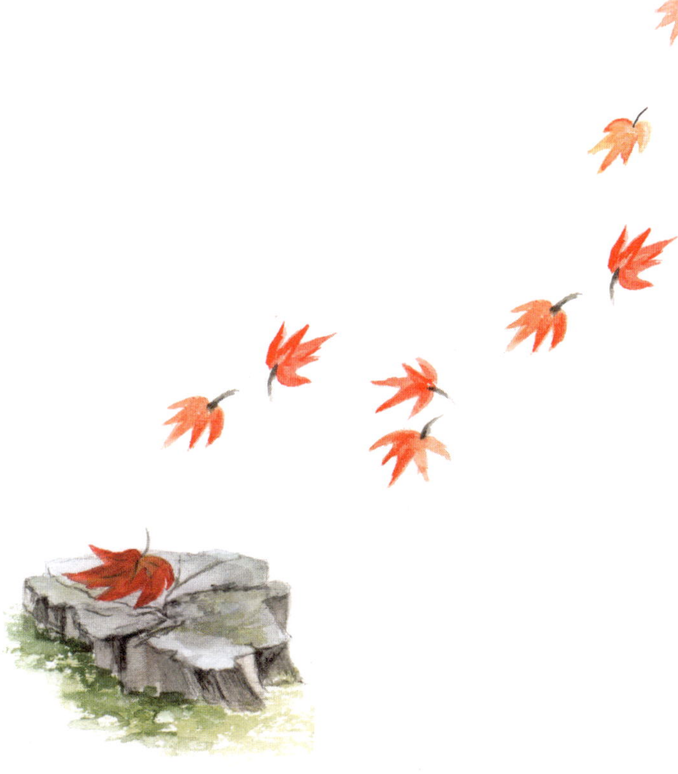

The Poems

A cat and its mate
with sad faces
at dawn.

有明にかこち顔也夫婦猫
Ariake ni kakochigao nari fufuneko

— ISSA

Even a dingy cat
has
a mate.

汚れ猫それでも妻は持にけり
Yogoreneko soredemo tsuma wa mochi ni keri

— ISSA

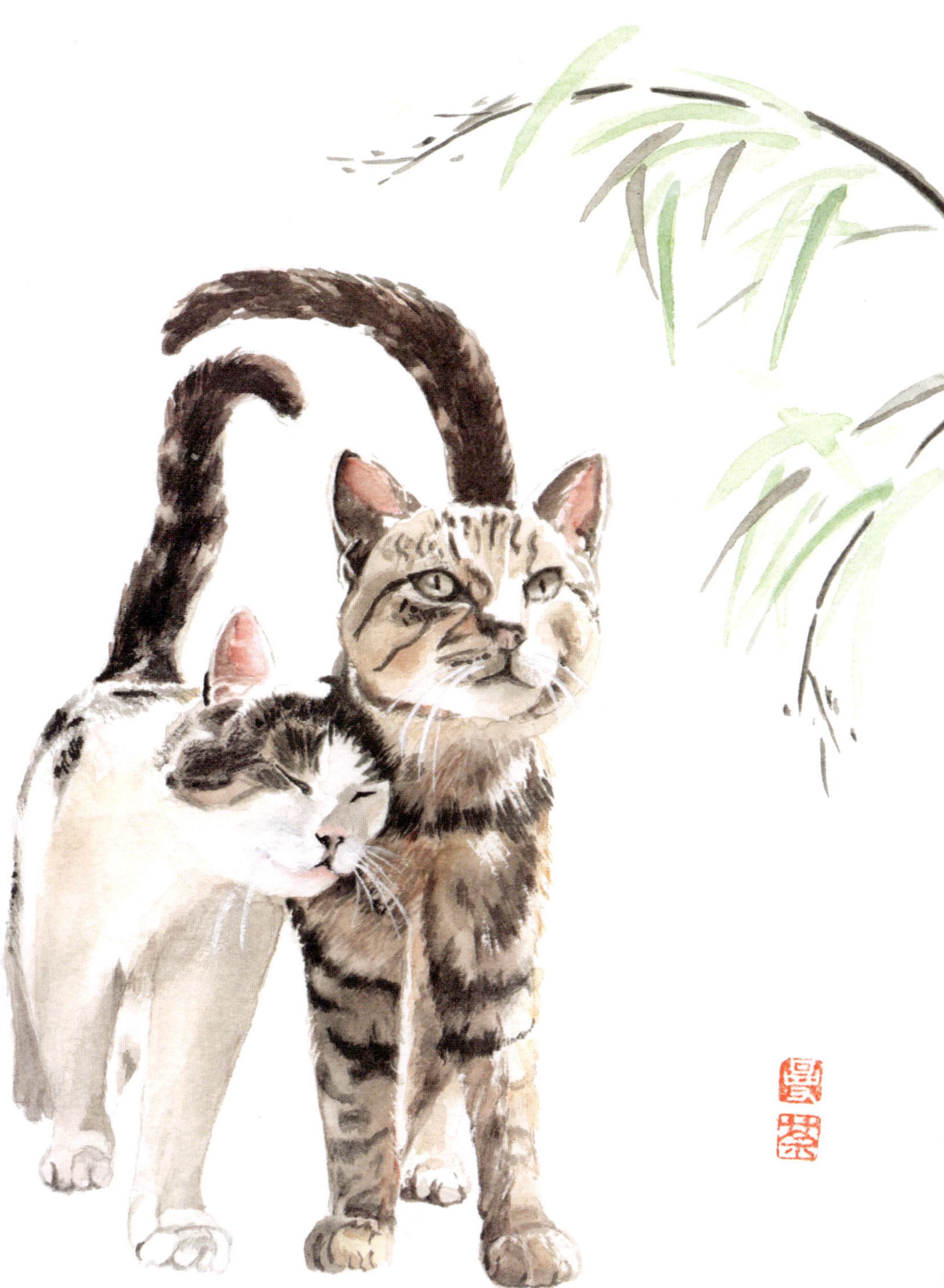

The cat's bell heard
throughout the long night;
chrysanthemums blooming.

猫の鈴夜永の菊の咲にけり

Neko no suzu yoei no kiku no saki ni keri

— ISSA

How pathetic!
Cats in love;
not a single mouse caught.

猫の恋鼠もとらず哀れなり

Neko no koi nezumi mo torazu aware nari

— HYAKURI

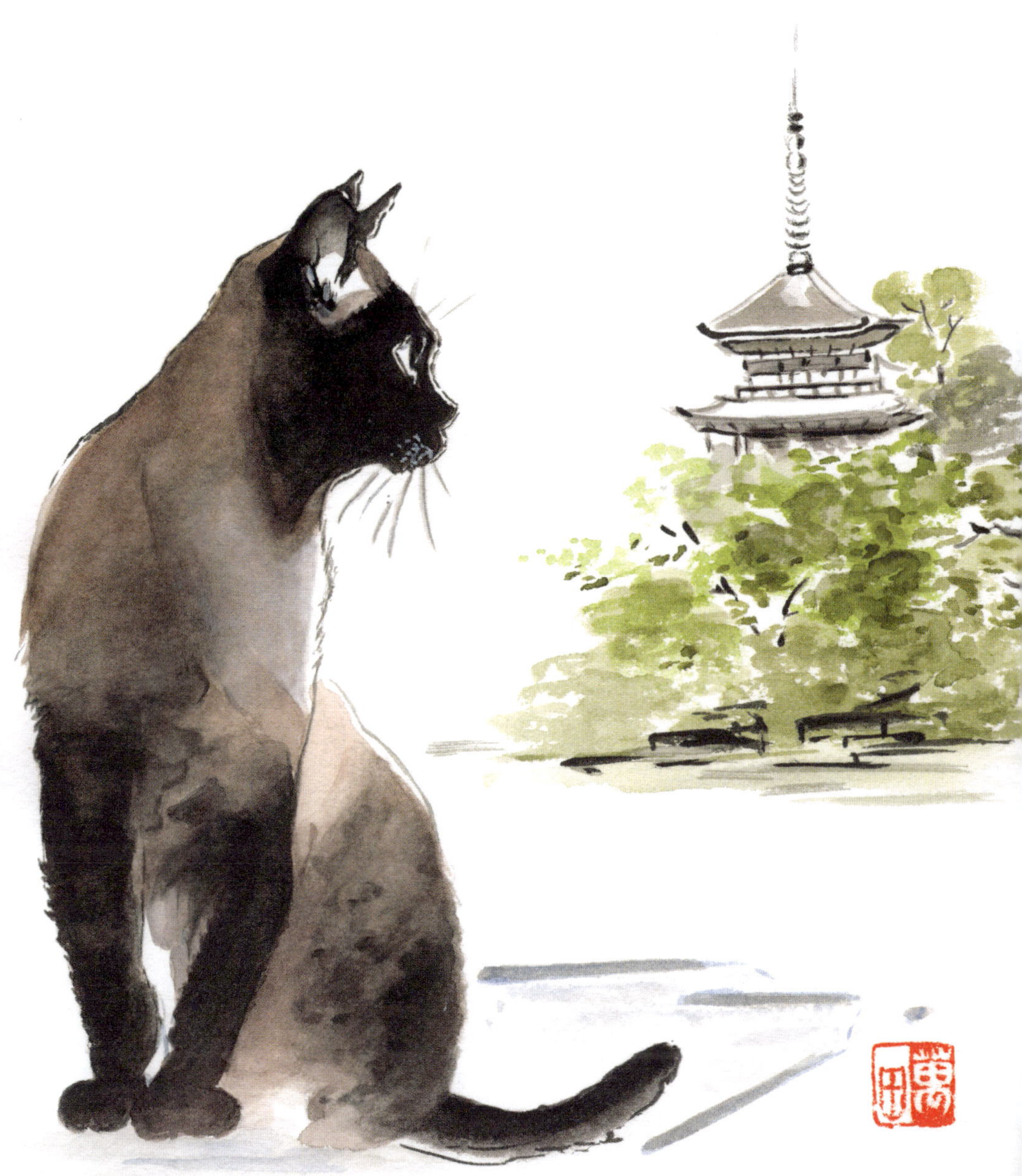

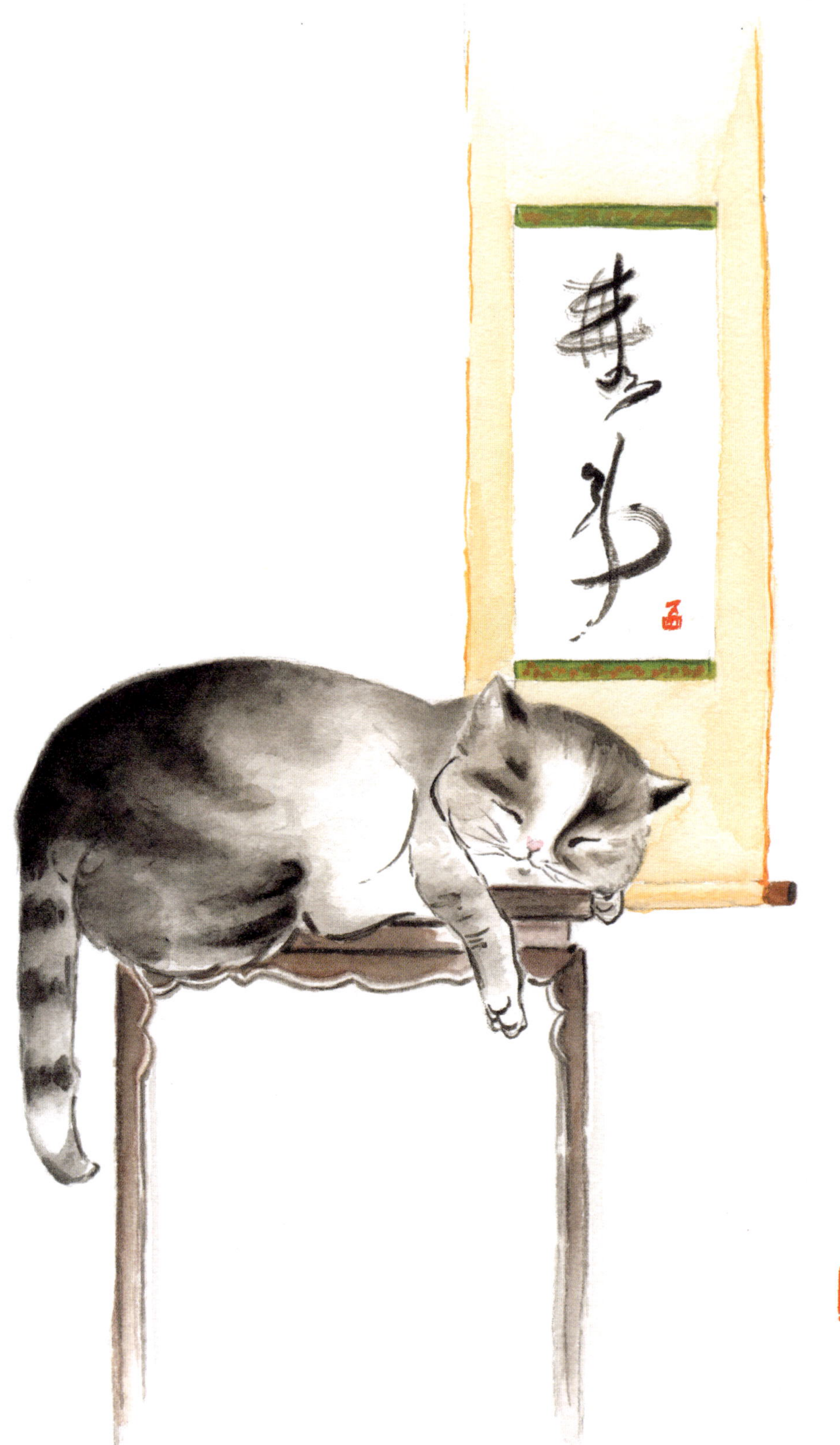

The large face of the cat
disappeared
from the window.

猫の大きな顔が窓から消えた
Neko no okina kao ga mado kara kieta

— HOSAI

Pretty fat,
and not scratching for fleas;
the back-country cat.

でくでくと蚤まけせぬや田舎猫
Dekudeku to nomimake senu ya inakaneko

— ISSA

Quiet, cicadas!
Master Whiskers
is here.

だまれ蝉今髭どのがござるそよ
Damare semi ima higedono ga gozaru so yo

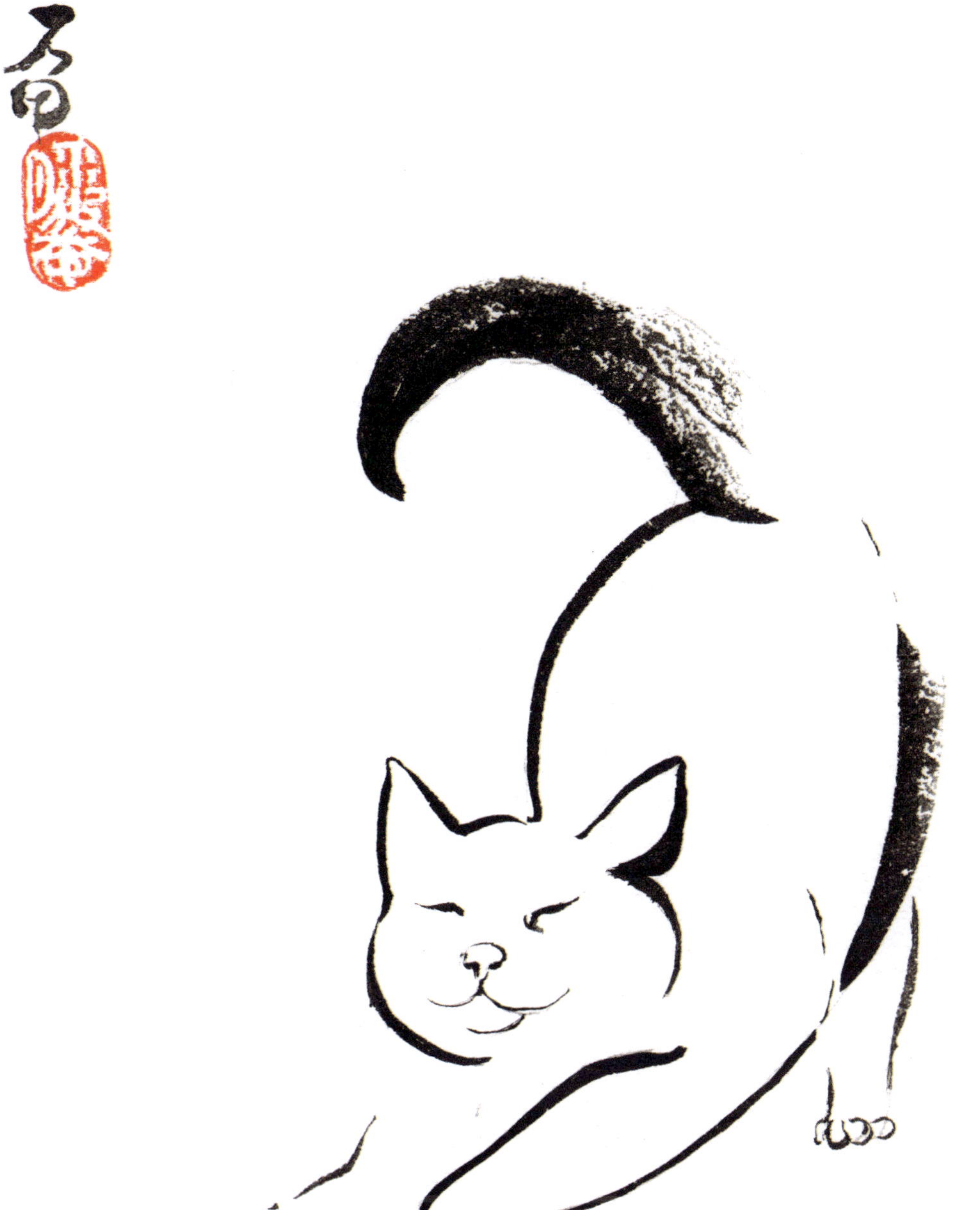

Slightly rearranging the doll shelf,
with a plop,
the kitten!

ひな棚にちよんと直りし小猫哉
Hinadana ni chon to naorishi koneko kana

— ISSA

On the branch, a nightingale!
In the lap of the Buddha,
a cat.

鶯や枝に猫は御ひざに
Uguisu ya eda ni neko wa gyo hiza ni

— ISSA

Pooping in the winter
garden:
the stray cat.

のら猫のふんしているや冬の庭
Nora neko no fun shite iru ya fuyu no niwa

— SHIKI

A night of frost;
opening the window to the cries
of an abandoned cat.

霜の夜や窓かいて鳴く勘当猫
Shimo no yo ya mado kaite naku kandoneko

— ISSA

Lying flat down,
full of shame,
the thieving cat.

恥入てひらたくなるやどろぼ猫
Hajiite hirataku naru ya dorobo neko

— ISSA

The cat passing by
right before my eyes;
not a sound.

わが目の前を通る猫の足音無し
Waga me no mae wo toru neko no ashioto nashi

— HOSAI

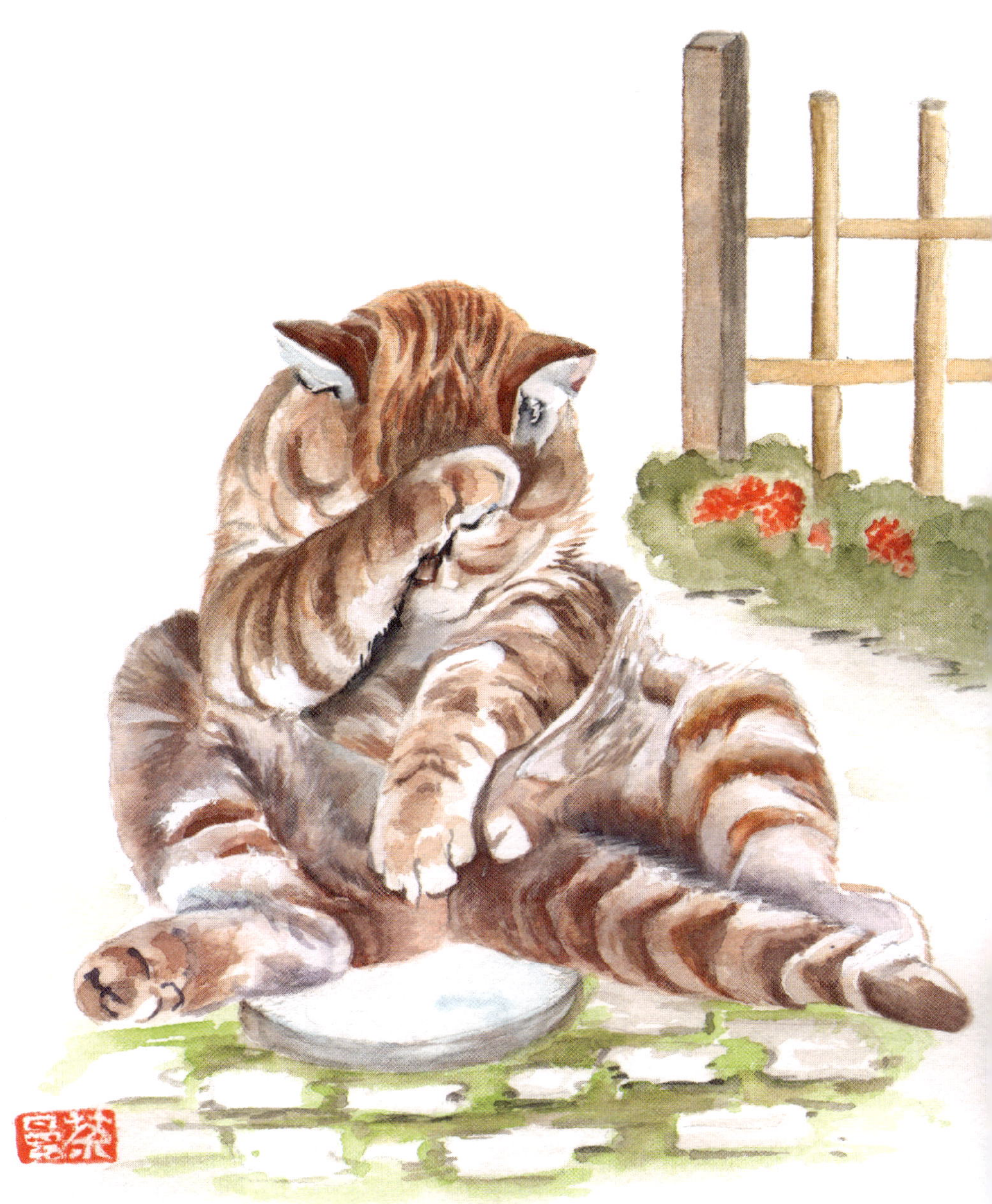

Biting the morning glory
with nonchalance
the cat.

ゆうがおの花かむ猫やよそごころ
Yugao no hana kamu neko ya yosogokoro

— BUSON

Cats in love,
both
with whiskers.

両方に口髭あるなり猫の恋
Ryoho ni kuchihige aru nari neko no koi

— RAIZAN

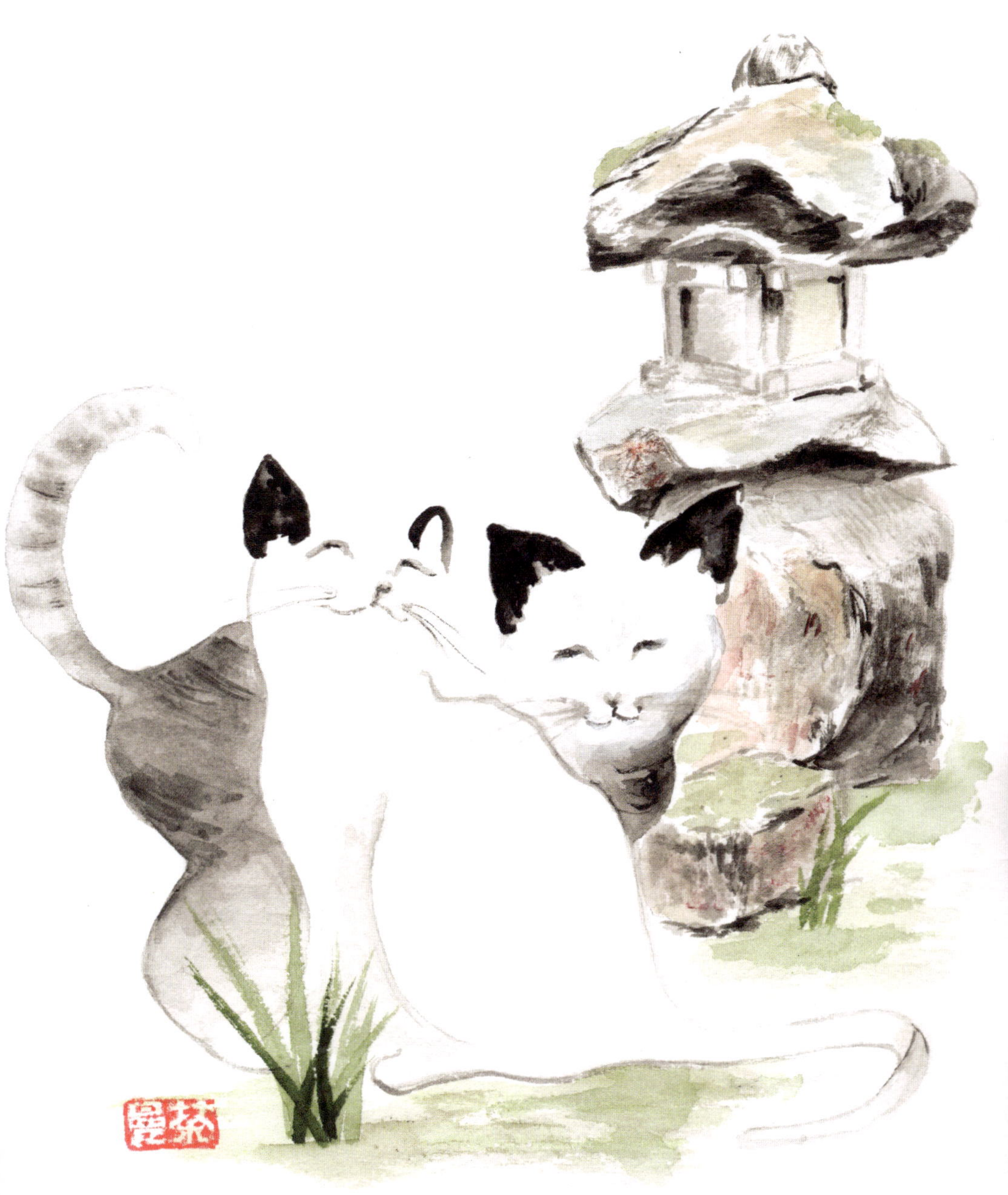

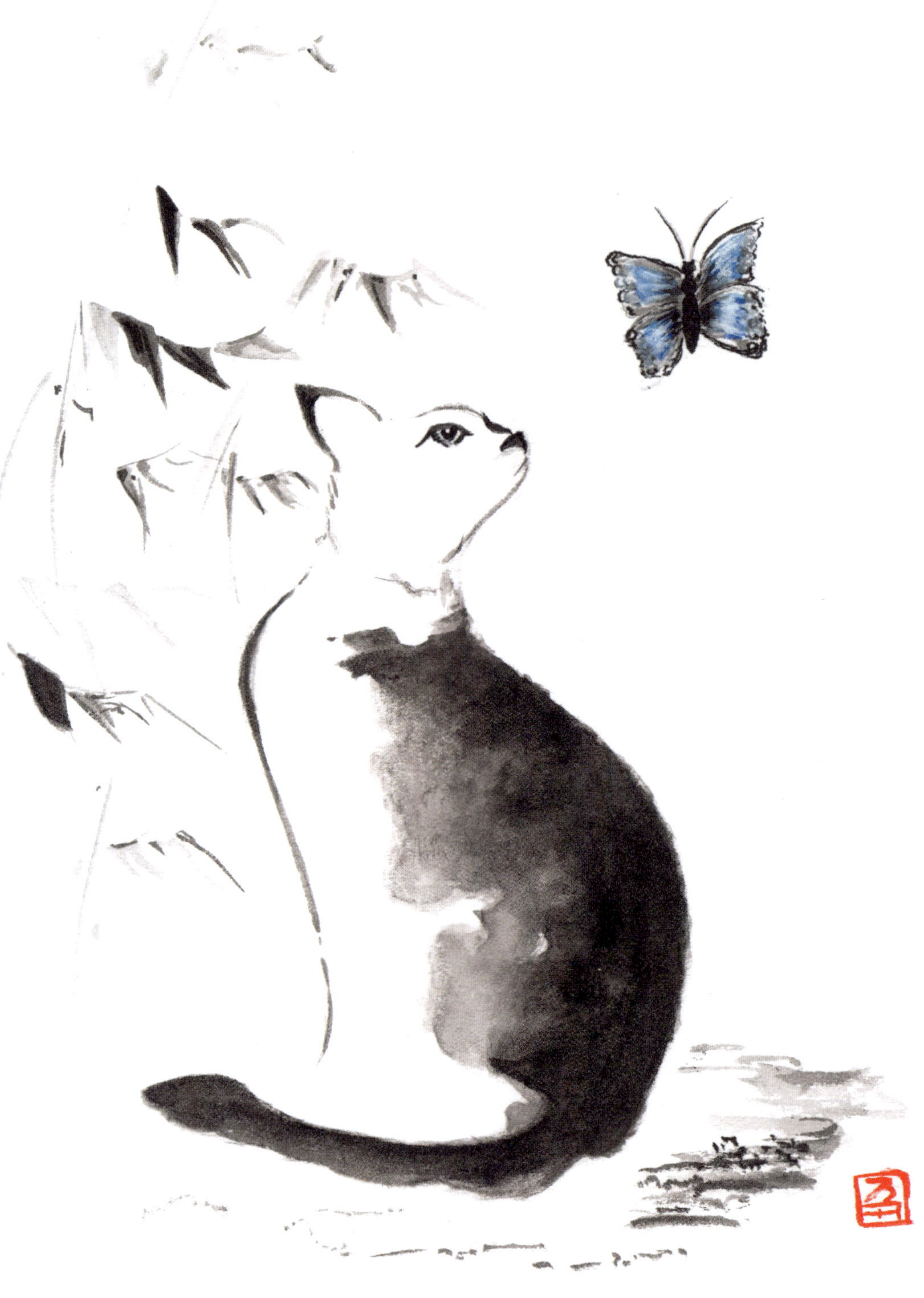

On the anniversary
of the kitten's death,
a little fluttering butterfly.

猫の子の命日をとぶ小蝶哉
Neko no ko no meinichi wo tobu kocho kana

— ISSA

The country cat
does nothing to swat
the fluttering butterfly.

まう蝶にふりも直さぬ野猫哉
Mau cho ni furi mo naosanu noneko kana

— ISSA

The passing year!
The cat hunches down
on my lap.

行く年や猫うずくまる膝の上
Yuku toshi ya neko uzukumaru hiza no ue

— SOSEKI

The king-size cat
flops down to sleep
on the paper fan.

大猫のどさりと寝たる団扇
Daineko no dosari to netaru uchiwa

— ISSA

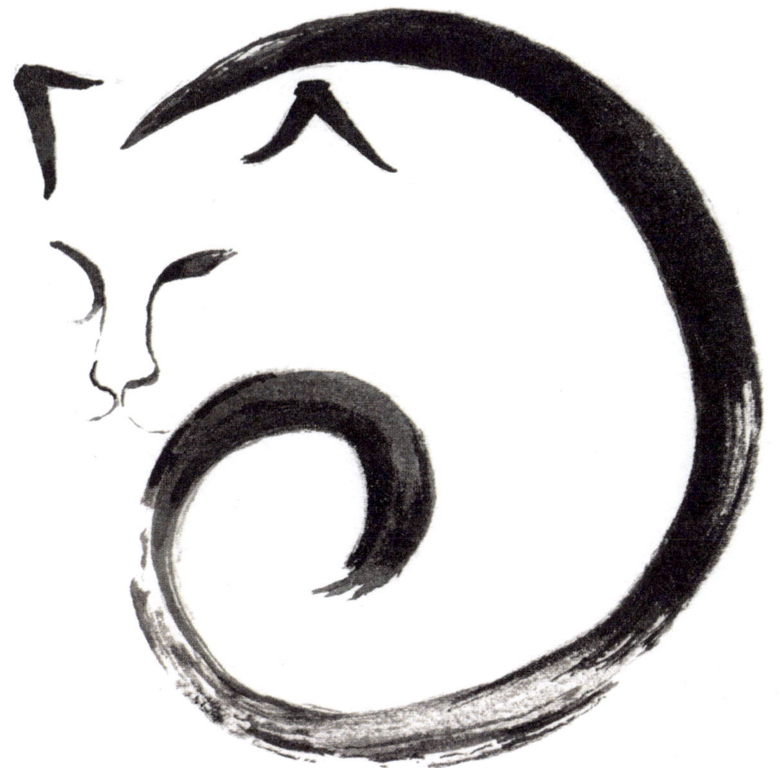

How frightening!
Sending stones flying from the steps:
cats in love.

おそろしさいしだん崩す猫のこい
Osoroshisa ishidan kuzusu neko no koi

— SHIKI

As a diversion
at the window,
a cat catching flies.

なぐさみに猫がとる也窓の蝿

Nagusami ni neko ga toru nari mado no hae

— ISSA

A high-spirited cat
skillfully jumping
over the flame.

火の上を上手にとぶはうかれ猫
Hi no ue wo jozu ni tobu wa ukare neko

— ISSA

In a deep dream
the cat stretches out
over the woman.

夢深き女に猫が背伸びせり
Yume fukaki onna ni neko ga senobi seri

— SANTOKA

Sleeping in a row:
butterflies, cats, and the temple's
chief priest.

寝並んで小蝶と猫と和尚哉
Nenarande kocho to neko to osho kana

— ISSA

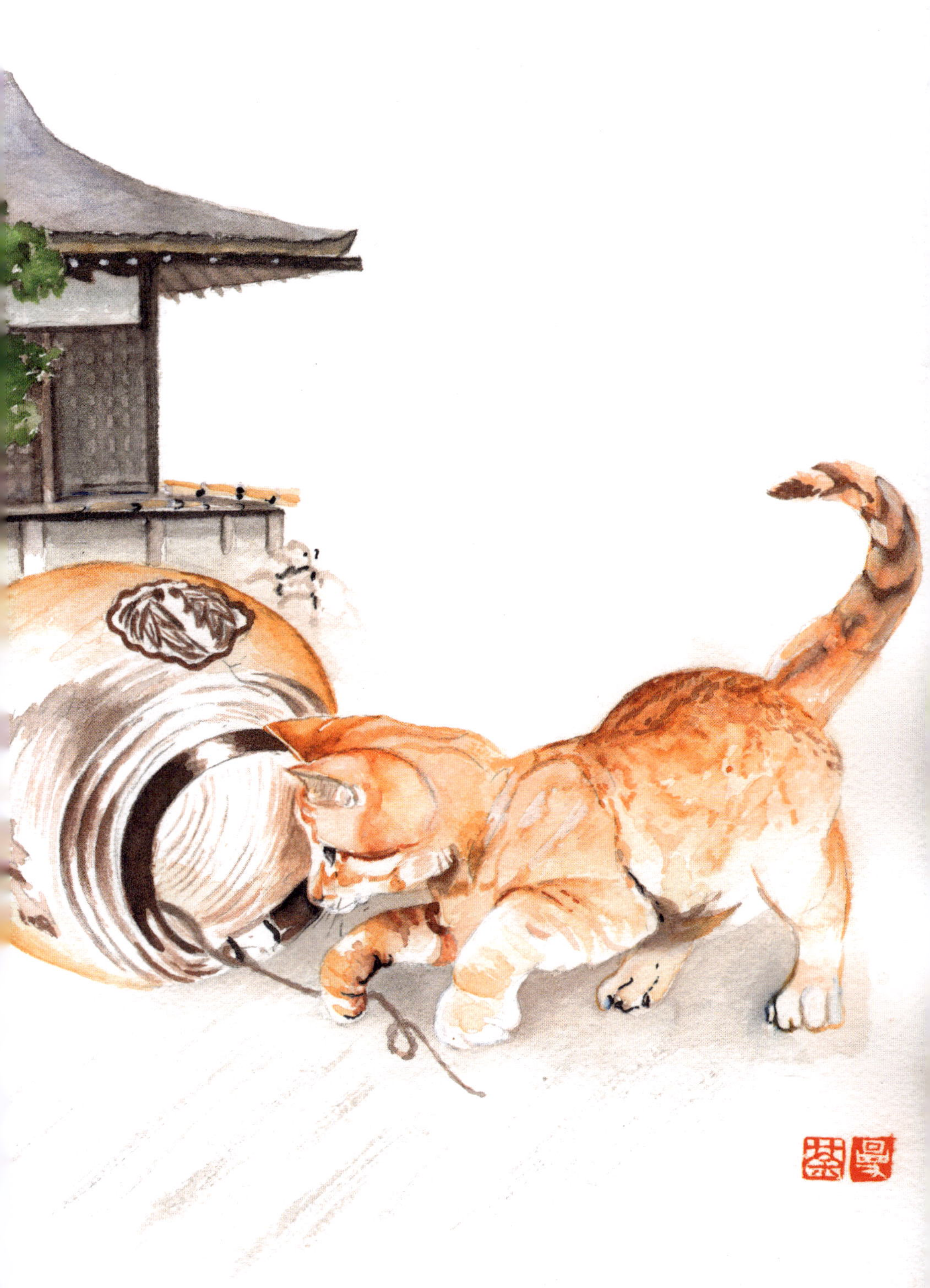

How I envy them!
When I've given up thoughts of love,
cats keep at it.

羨やまし思ひきるとき猫の恋
Urayamashi omoikiru toki neko no koi

— ETSUJIN

All night long,
cats, too, keeping one eye open;
looking for love.

夜すがらや猫も人目を忍恋
Yosugara ya neko mo hitome wo shinobu koi

— ISSA

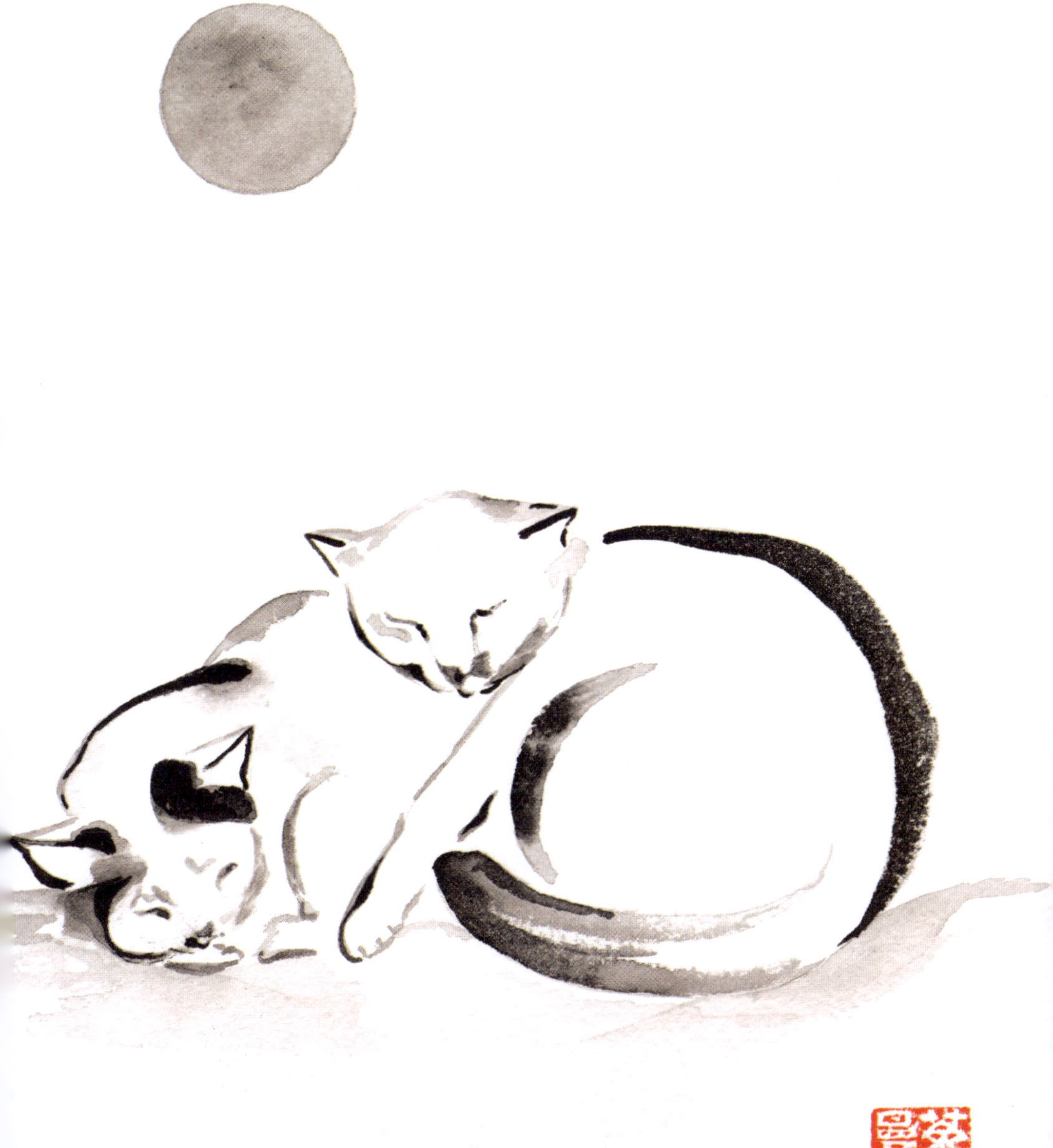

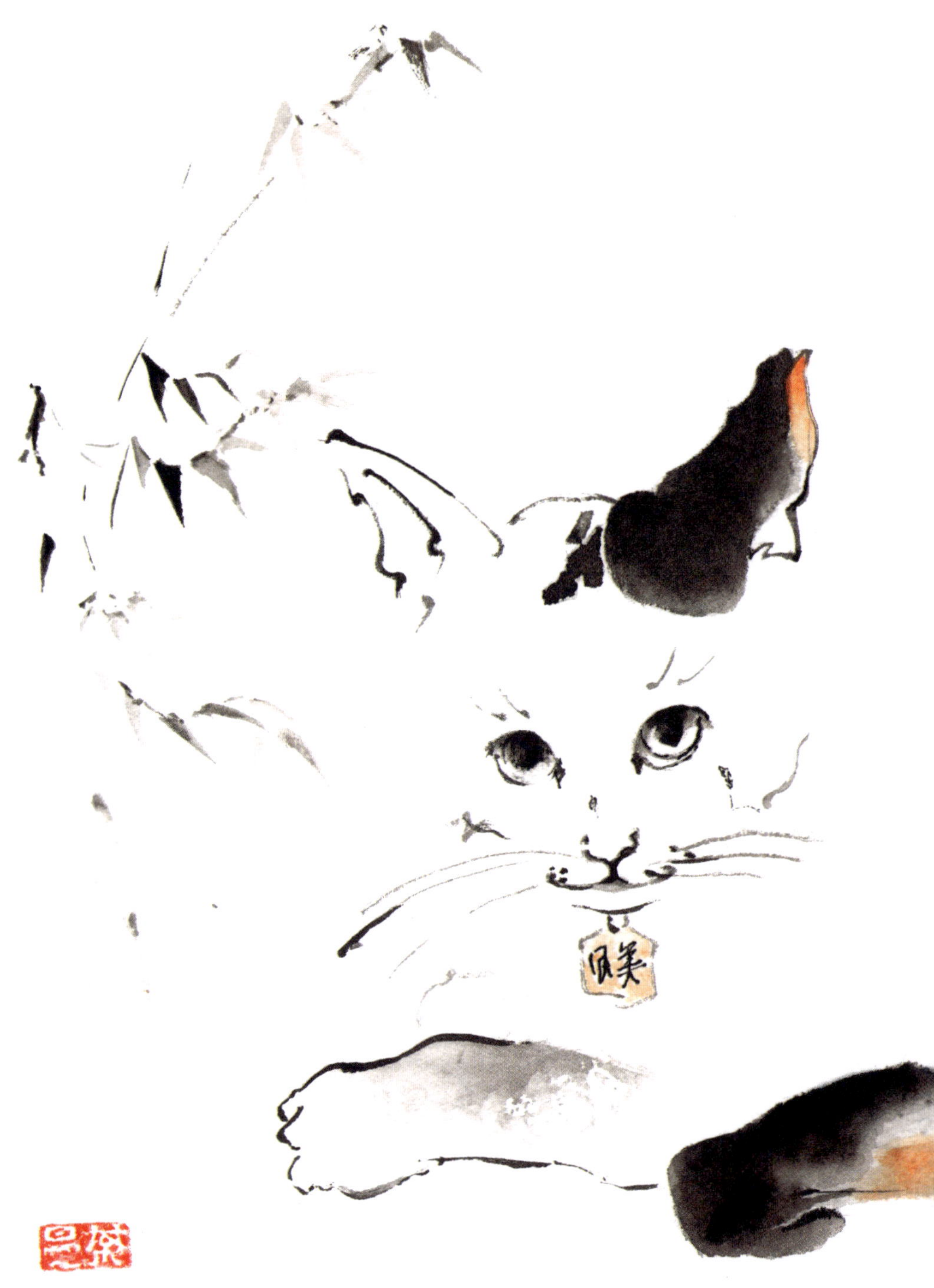

In the shadow
of the morning glory leaves;
a cat's eyes?

朝顔の葉陰に猫の眼玉かな
Asagao no hakage ni neko no medama kana

— SOSEKI

The kitten
dancing round and round
amidst falling leaves.

猫の子のくるくる舞ひやちる木のは
Neko no ko no kurukuru mai ya chiru ko no ha

— ISSA

The cats, too,
sitting among the others, the year end
drinking party.

御仲間に猫も坐とるや年わすれ
O-nakama ni neko mo zatoru ya toshi wasure

— F U S E I

The mother cat
steals something for her kitten
and runs.

女猫子ゆへの盗みとく逃
Onna neko ko yue no nusumi toku nigeru

— I S S A

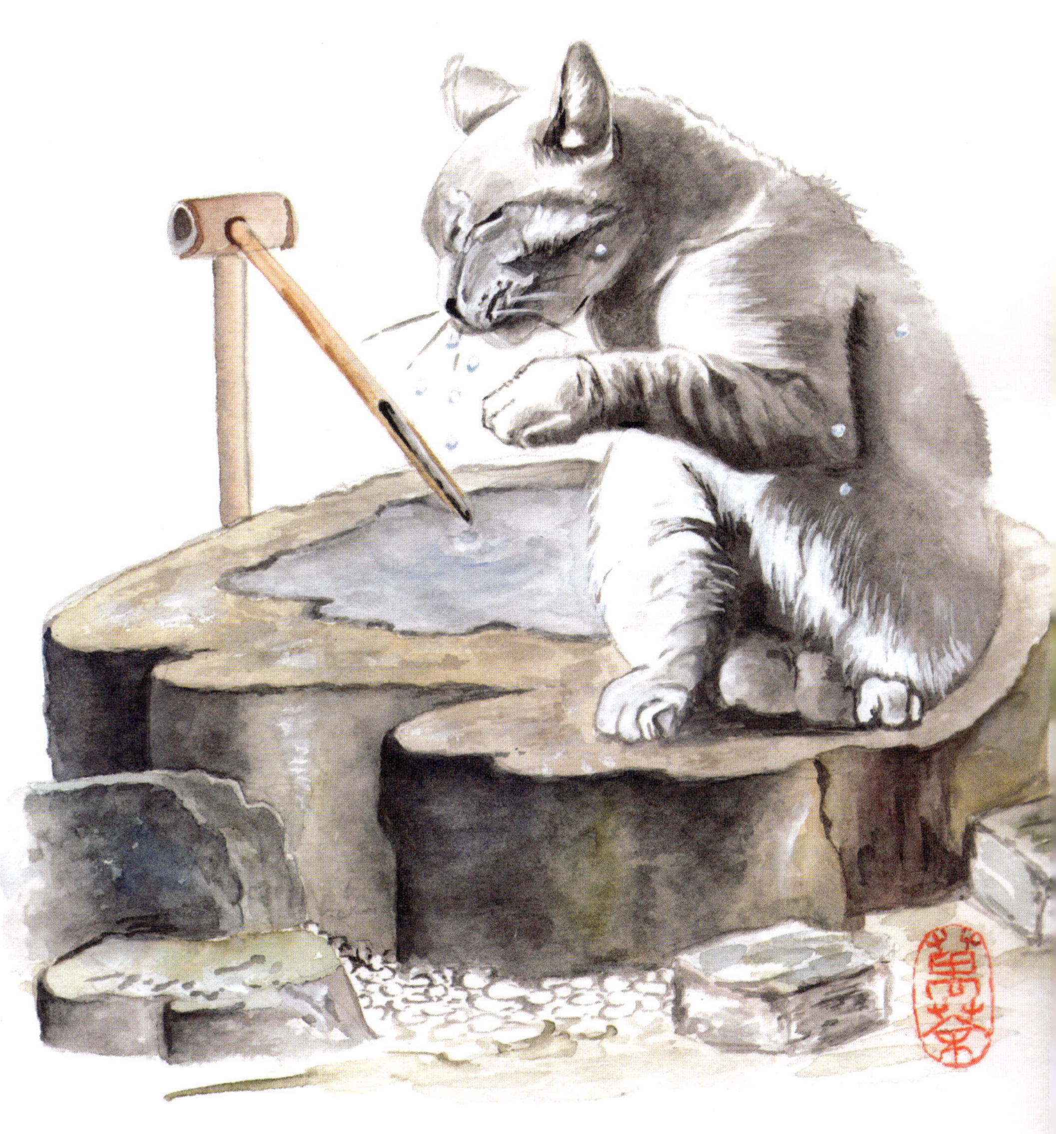

In the meadow
scratching away;
fleas on the cat.

草原にこすり落や猫の蚤
Kusahara ni kosuriotosu ya neko no nomi

— ISSA

Up comes the cat
rustling
the banana plant.

かさがさと猫のあがりし芭蕉かな
Kasagasa to neko no agarishi basho kana

— SHIKI

The butterfly is gone,
but the kitten still
crouches in wait.

蝶去ってまた蹲据る子猫かな
Cho satte mata uzukumaru koneko kana

— SOSEKI

Lovemaking cats
abruptly
going their ways.

猫の恋打切棒ニ別レけり
Neko no koi bukkiribo ni wakare keri

— ISSA

Master Whiskers is coming!
So, geese in the rice paddy,
Quiet down!

髭殿がおじゃるぞだまれ小田鴈

Higedono ga ojaru zo damare oda no kari

— ISSA

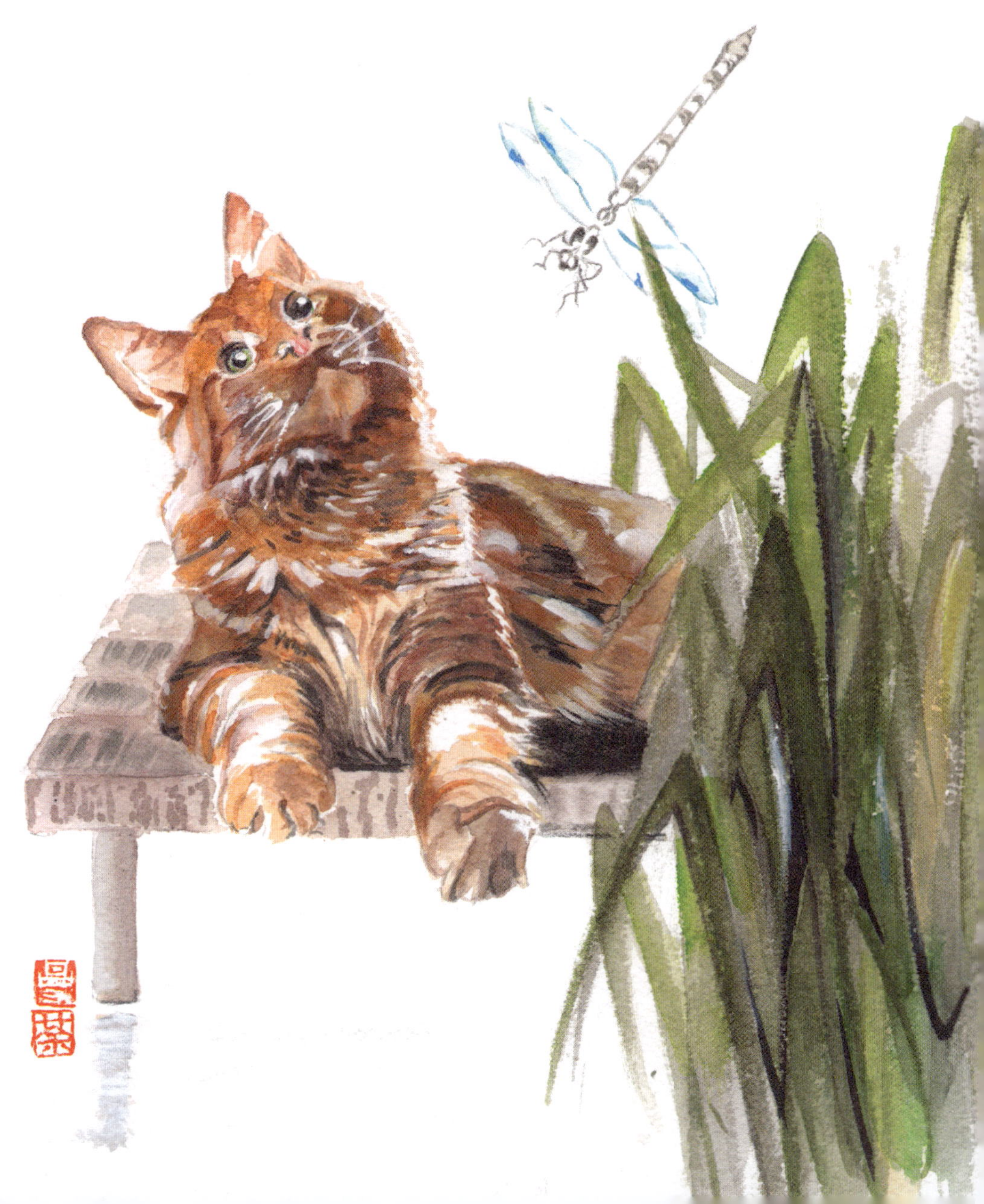

Sharing the ball
with the kitten
to play.

猫の子にかして遊ばす手まり哉
Neko no ko ni kashite asobasu temari kana

— ISSA

Hanging on the weighing scales,
it keeps on playing:
the kitten.

猫の子や秤ニかかりつつざれる
Neko no ko ya hakari ni kakari tsutsu zareru

— ISSA

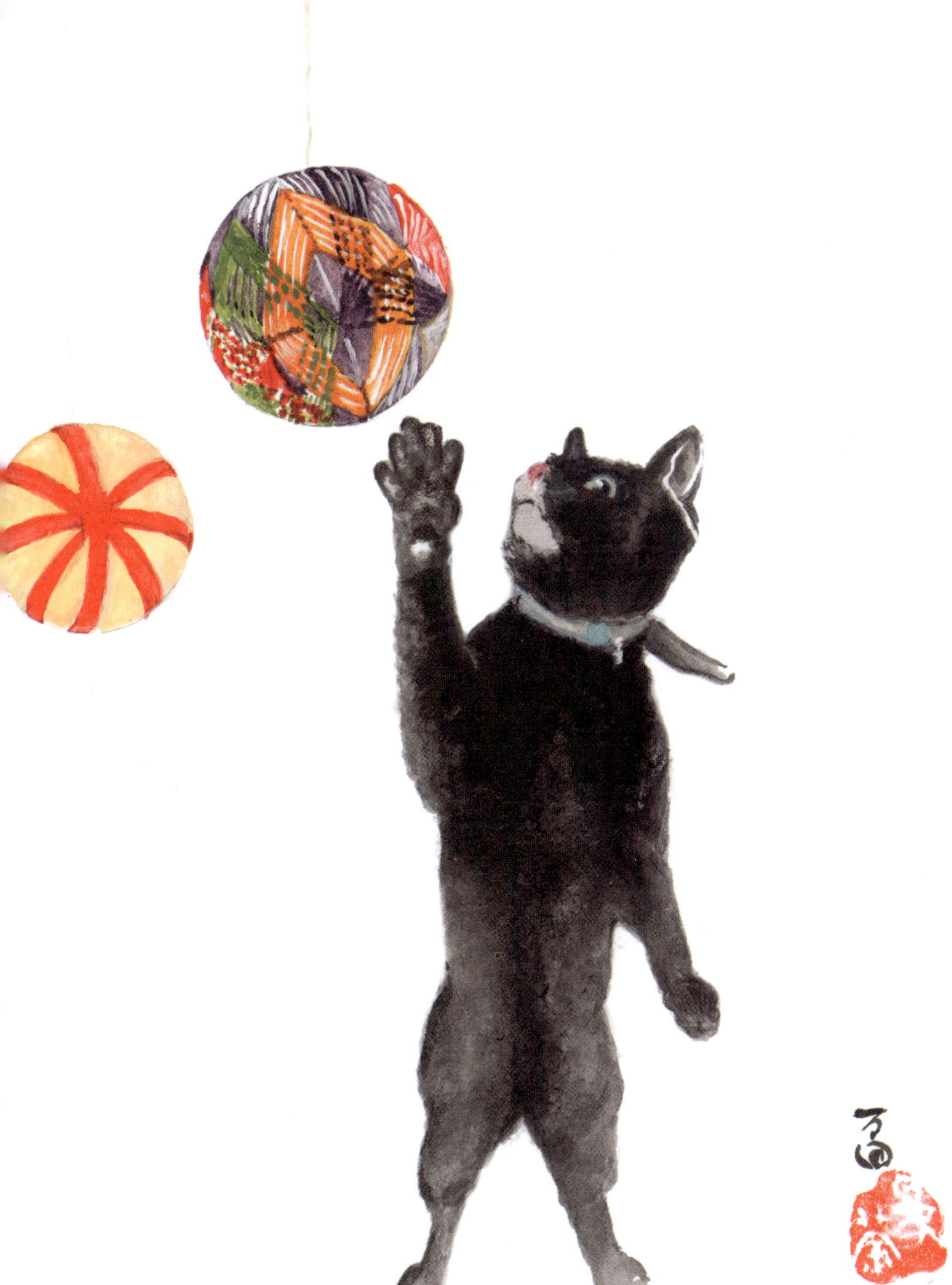

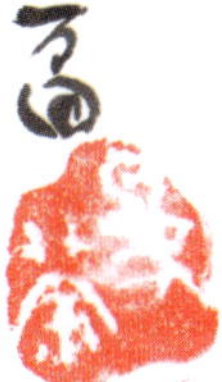

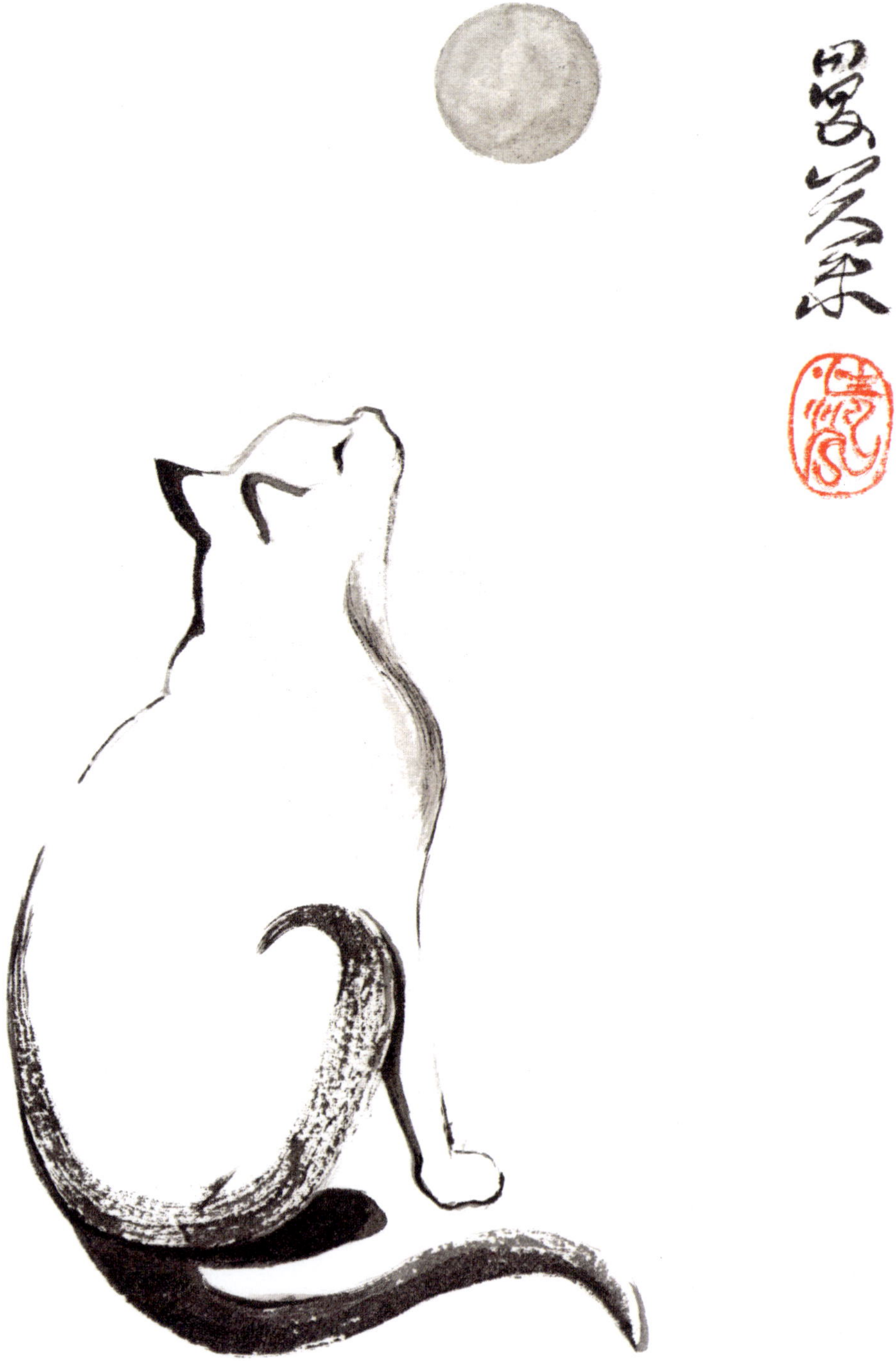

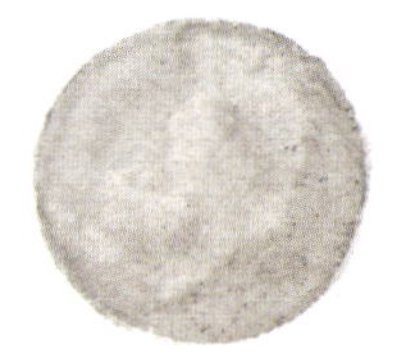
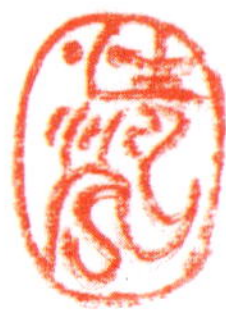

Cats making love;
when they quit,
the bedroom's hazy moon.

猫の恋やむとき閨の朧月

Neko no koi yamu toki neya no oborotsuki

— BASHO

Turning its head, putting on airs,
licking itself,
a cat in the moonlight.

頭をふりて身をなめよそふ月の猫

Atama wo furite mi wo name yo so tsuki no neko

— KUSATAO

Simmering heat!
The cat snores
in deep breaths.

陽炎にくいくい猫の鼾哉
Kagero ni kuikui neko no ibiki kana

— ISSA

Cats making love,
then, nothing;
a moonlit night.

恋猫の又してもなく月夜かな
Koi neko no mata shite mo naku tsukiyo kana

— SEIGETSU

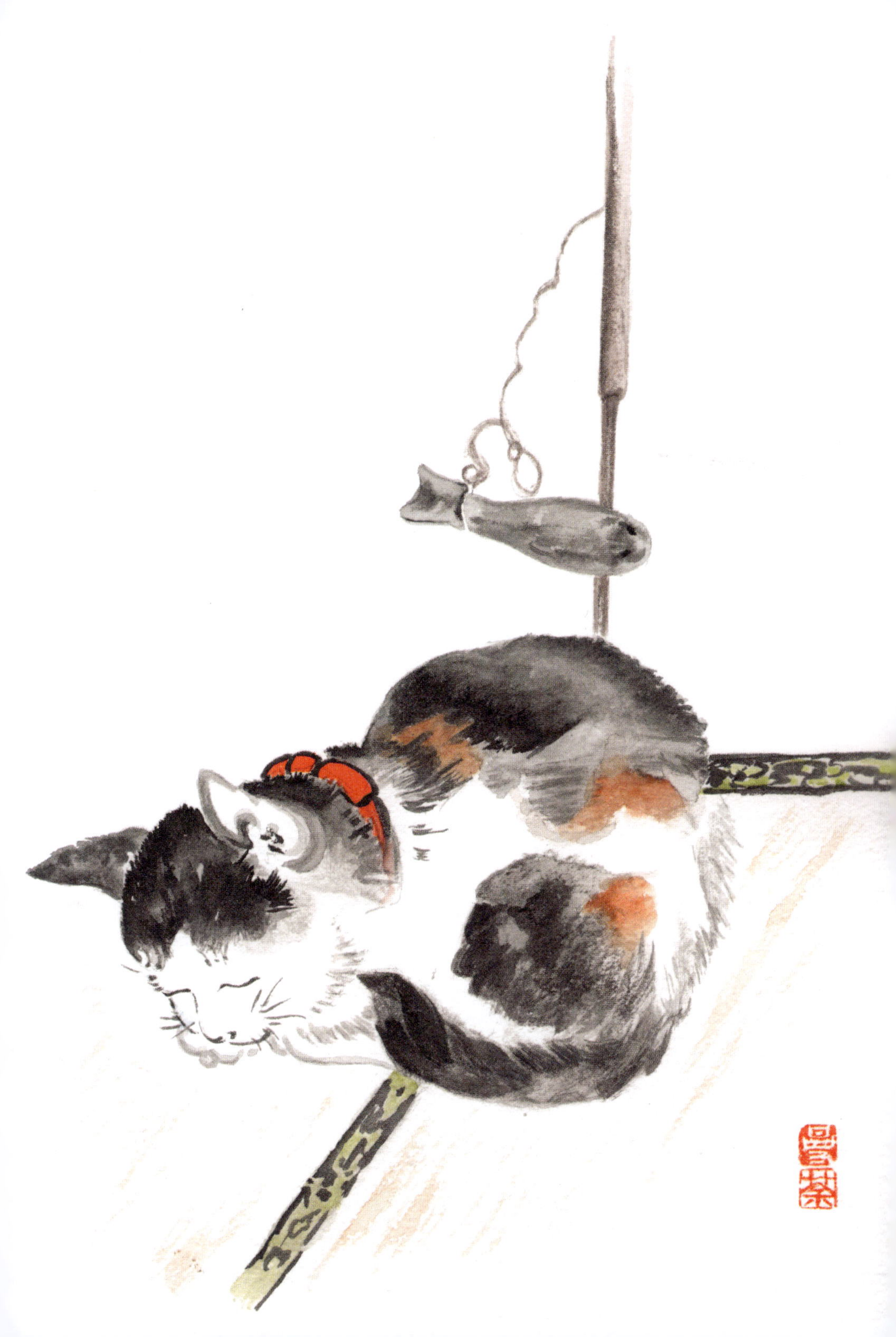

The stream on a moonlit night;
a cat comes to drink.
I'll have some, too.

月夜の水を猫が来て飲む私も飲まう
Tsukiyo no mizu wo neko ga kite nomu
watakushi mo nomo

— SANTOKA

Waves of heat
effortless down the verandah,
a sleepy cat.

陽炎や縁からころり寝ぼけ猫
Kagero ya en kara korori neboke neko

— ISSA

Cats in love;
thinning out,
just their eyes.

恋猫の眼ばかりに痩せにけり
Koi neko no me bakari ni yase ni keri

— SOSEKI

Teased by the tail
of a big cat,
the butterfly.

大猫の尻尾でなぶる小蝶哉
Oneko no shippo de naburu kocho kana

— ISSA

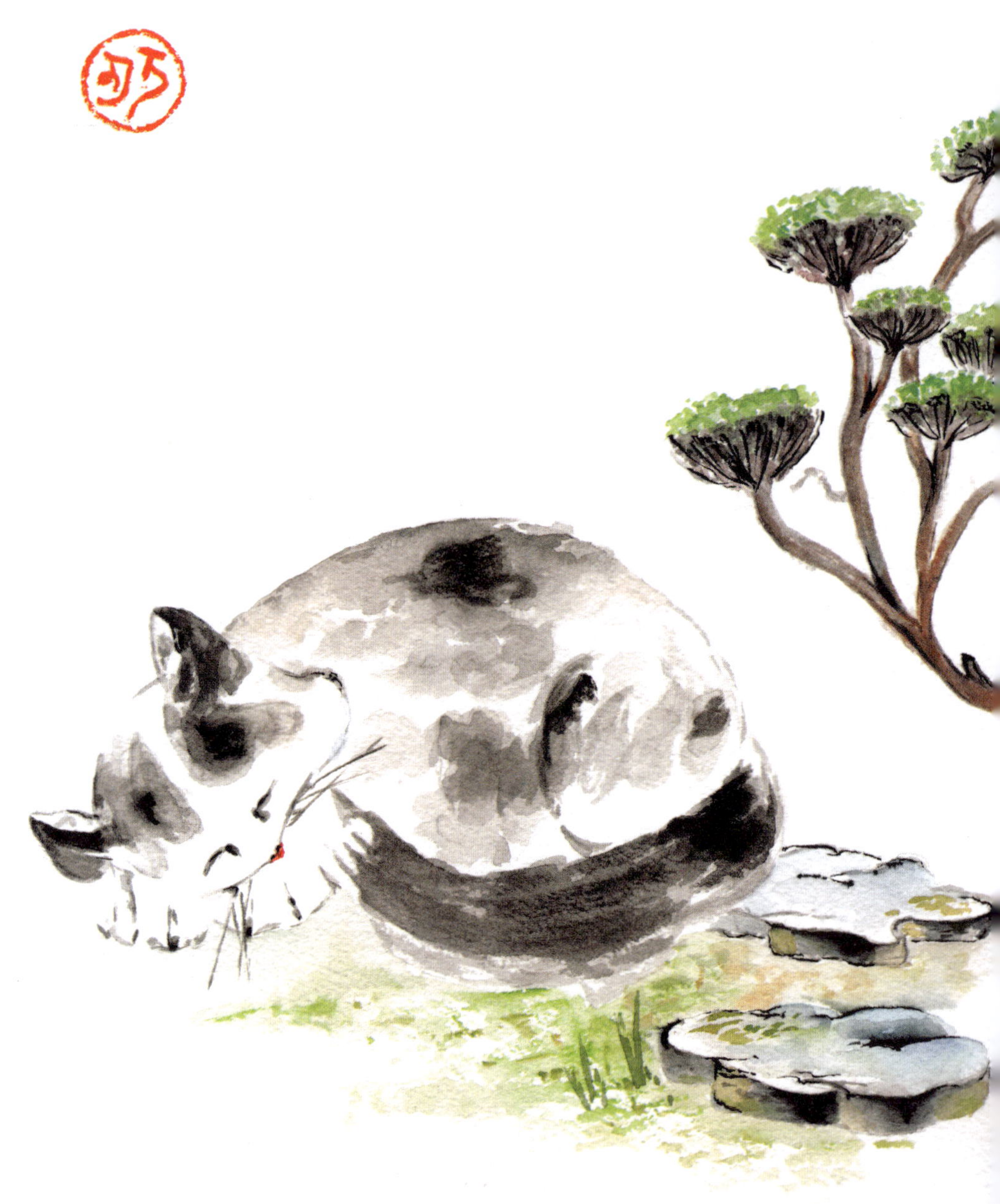

The lazy cat
pricks up its ears,
then, asleep again.

不性猫きき耳立て又眠る
Busho neko kikimimi tatete mata nemuru

Hidden by the leaves,
a cucumber for a pillow,
a kitten.

葉がくれの瓜を枕二子猫哉
Hagakure no uri wo makura ni koneko kana

A kitten,
dancing round and round
in falling leaves.

猫の子のくるくる舞ひやちる木のは
Neko no ko no kurukuru mai ya chiru ko no ha

— ISSA

Leaves falling in the wind, gently
pinning them down,
the kitten.

風のおち葉ちょいちょい猫が押へけり
Kaze no ochiba choi choi neko ga osaekeri

— ISSA

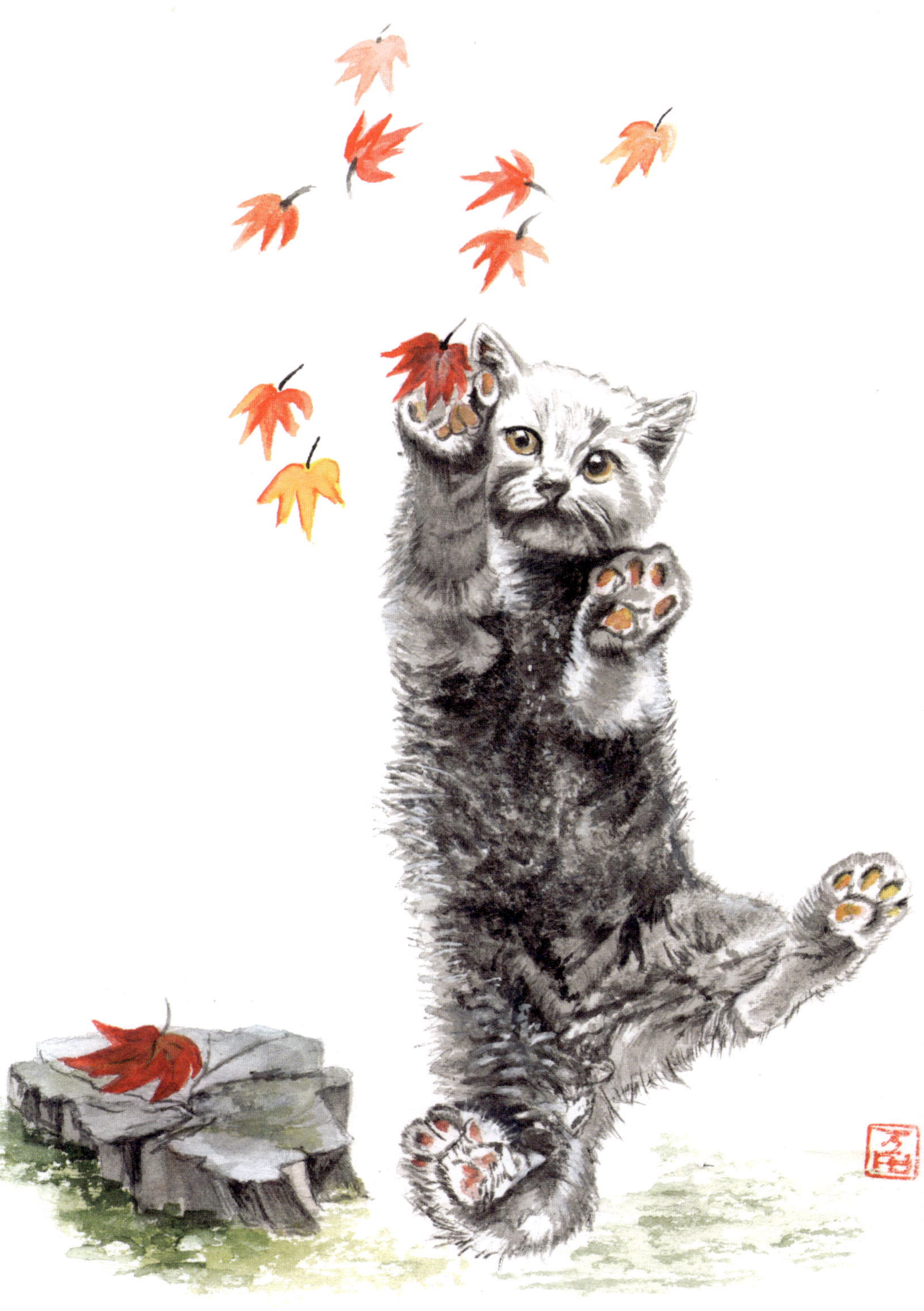

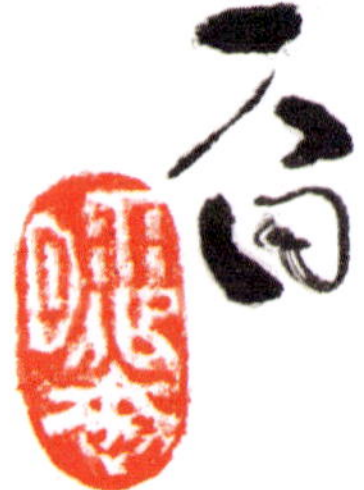

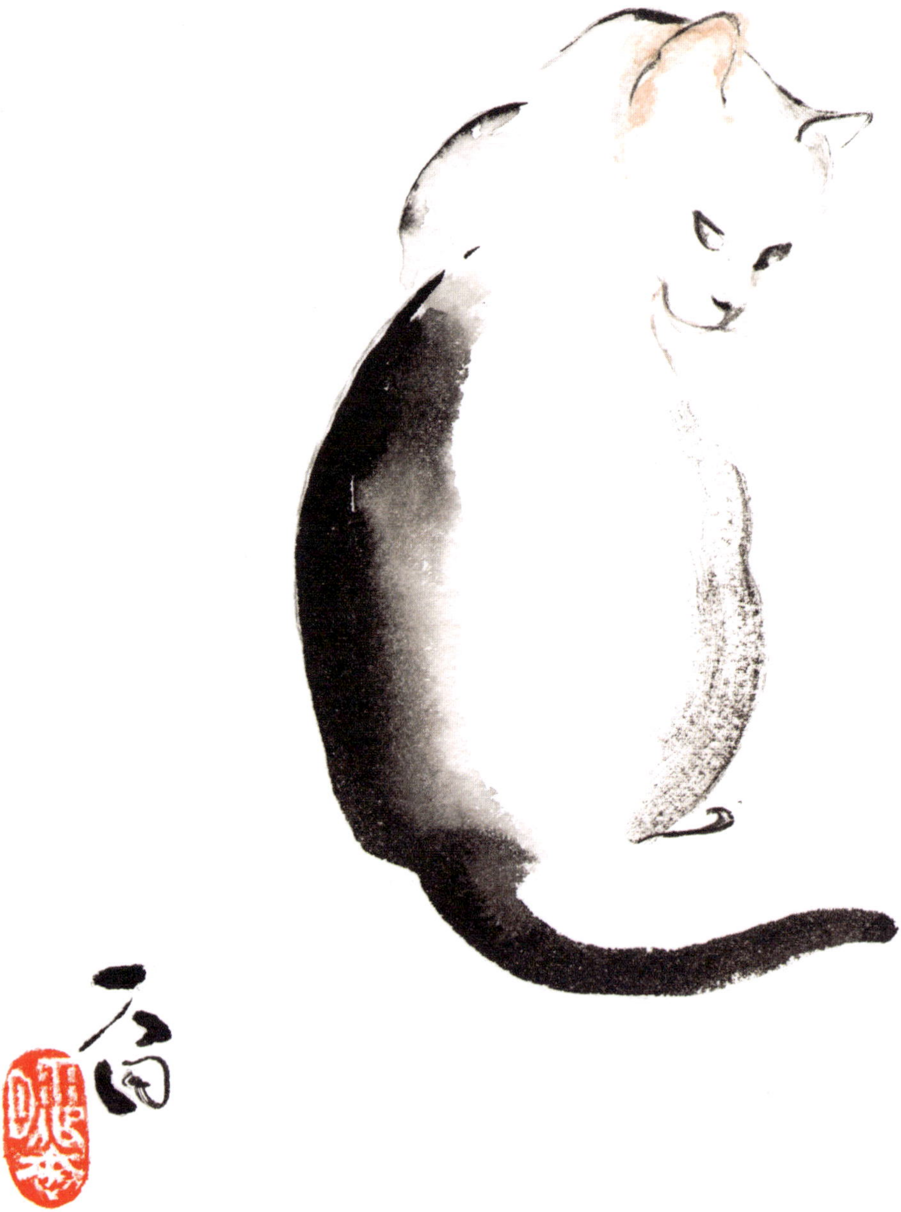

The snake's head leaving
the hole, the cat
gets ready.

あなを出る蛇の頭や猫が張る
Ana wo deru hebi no atama ya neko ga haru

— ISSA

I was the one
catching the eye
of the thieving cat.

どろぼう猫の眼とあってる自分であった
Dorobo neko no me to atteru jibun de atta

— HOSAI

A stray cat
coming out from the eaves;
a winter moon.

のら猫のかけ出す軒や冬の月
Nora neko no kakedasu noki ya fuyu no tsuki

— JOSO

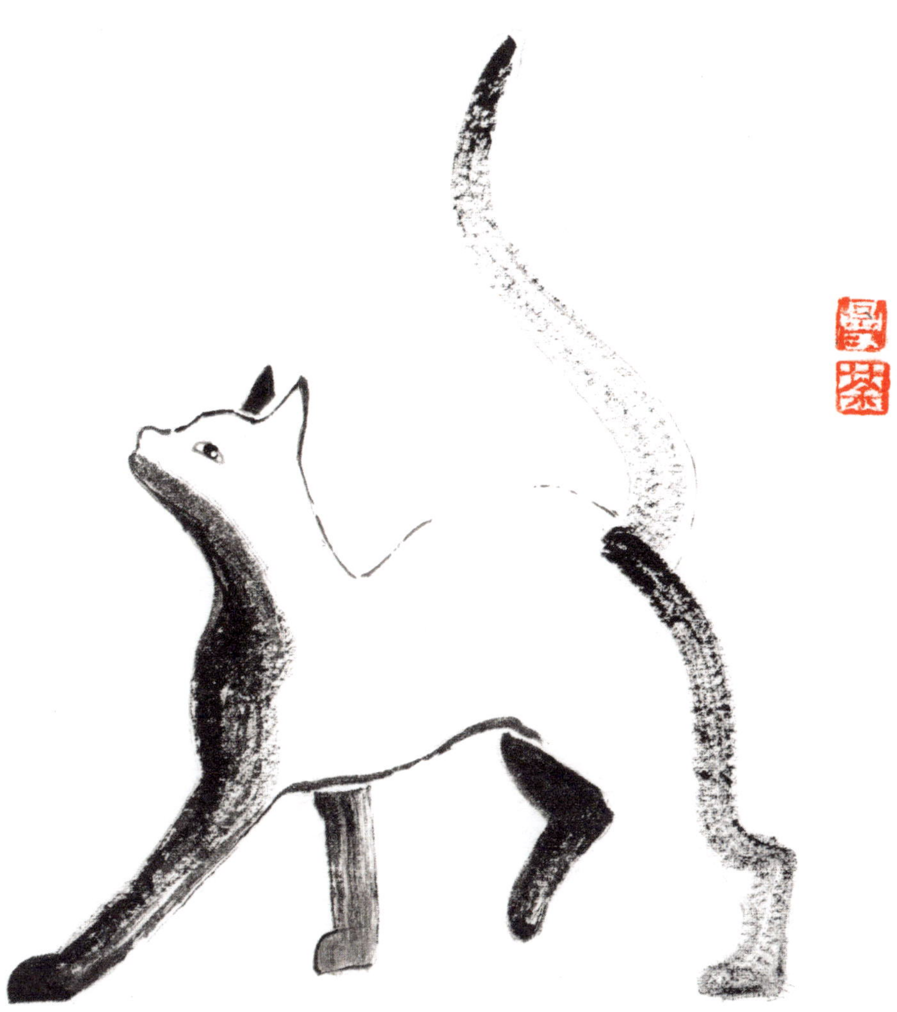

Sleeping, waking up;
a big long yawn;
cats in love.

寝て起て大欠して猫の恋
Nete okite oakubi shite neko no koi

— ISSA

The cat's eyes,
not yet noon,
a spring day.

猫の目のまだ昼過ぬ春日かな
Neko no me no mada hiru suginu haruhi kana

— ONITSURA

Master whiskers
gets up stretching, stretching;
the cry of a pheasant.

髭どのを伸上りつつきじの鳴
Higedono wo nobiagari tsutsu kiji no naku

— ISSA

The cat's bell
here and there
among the peonies.

猫の鈴ぼたんのあっちこっち哉
Neko no suzu botan no atchi kotchi kana

— ISSA

Even a stray cat
knows its own
bed.

安房猫おのがふとんは知にけり
Anbo neko ono ga futon wa shiri ni keri

— ISSA

Plum flowers blooming!
On the paper screen
the cat's silhouette.

梅咲やせうじに猫の影法師
Ume saku ya shoji ni neko no kageboshi

— ISSA

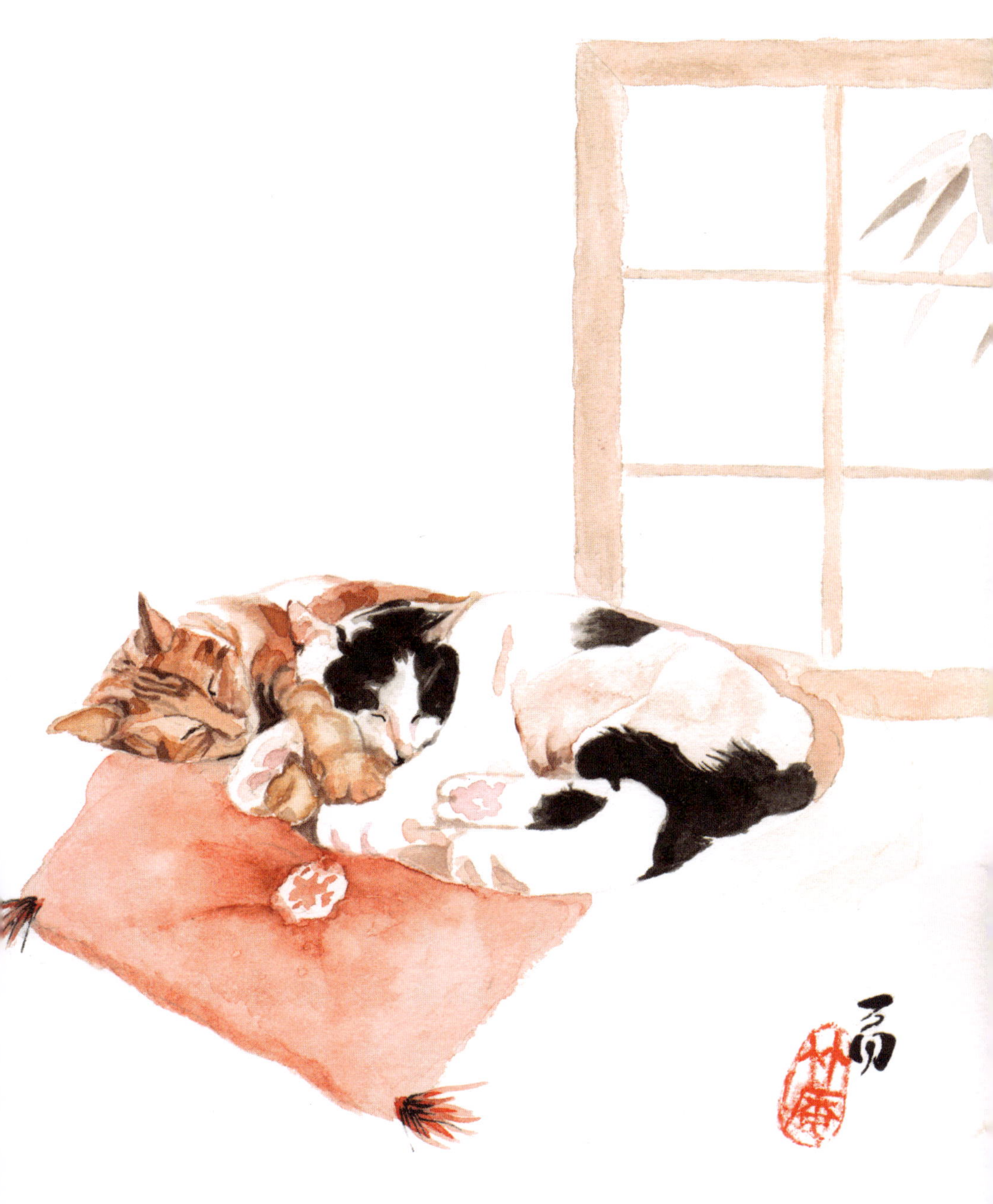

Late autumn shower;
coming to greet me,
my hermitage's cat.

時雨るるや迎に出たる庵の猫
Shigururu ya mukae ni detaru io no neko

— ISSA

A cat on a spree
comes along strangely
impatient.

うかれ猫奇妙ニ焦て参りけり
Ukare neko kimyo ni jirete mairi keri

— ISSA

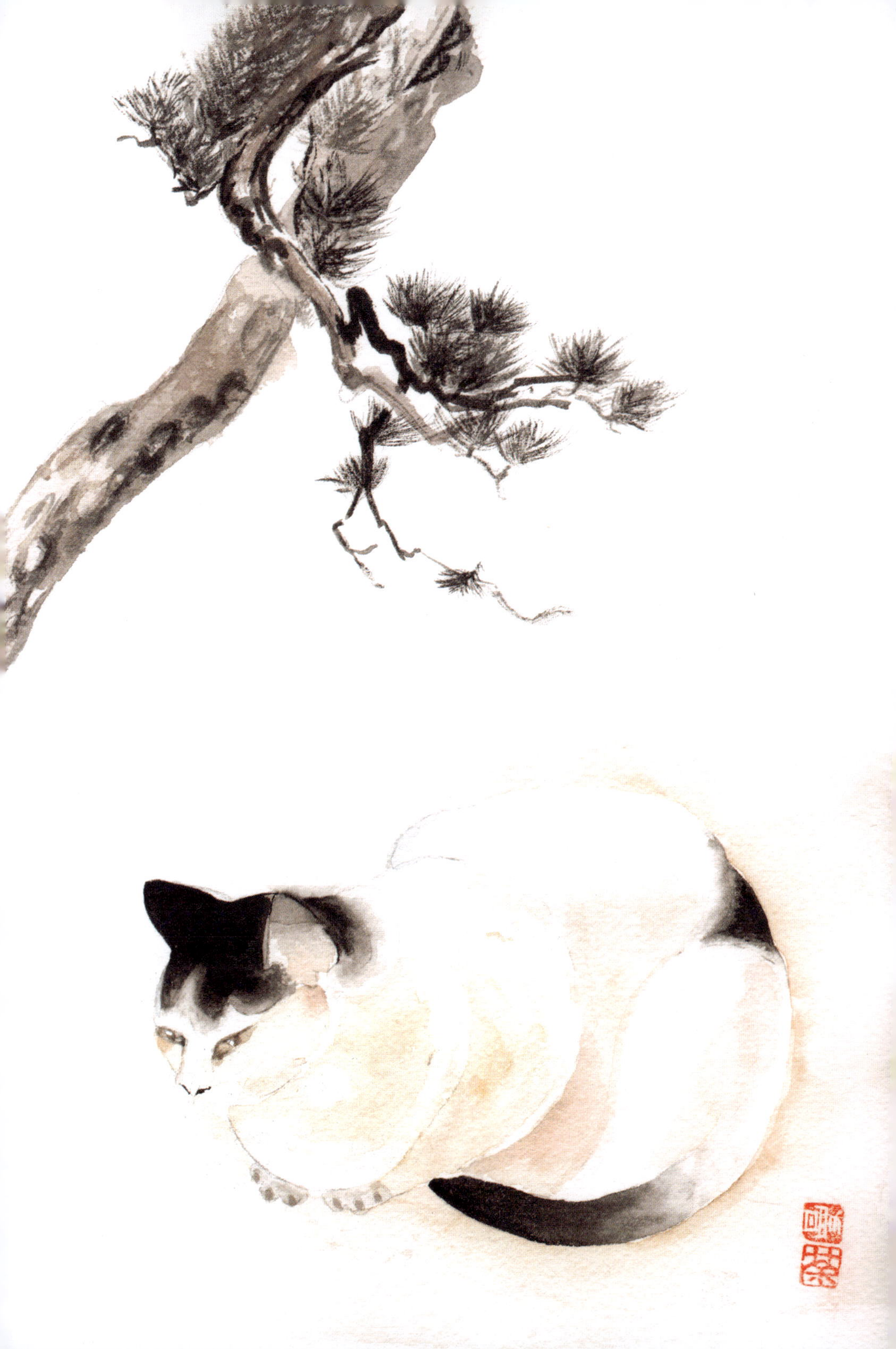

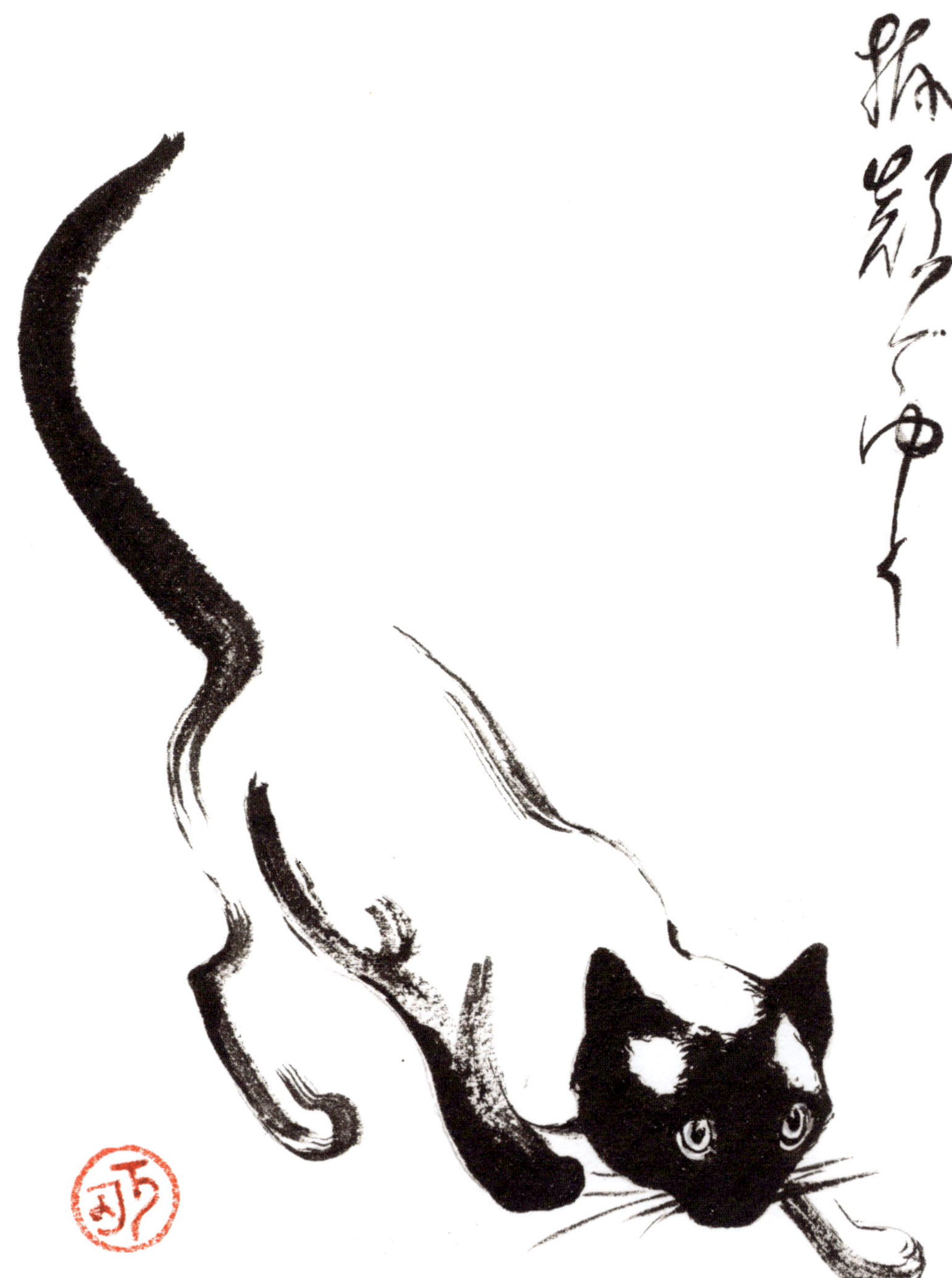

Slinking lower and lower,
a cat goes through
bush clover.

背を低め低め猫ゆく首蓿
Se wo hikume hikume neko yuku umagoyashi

— HASHIMOTO

From beneath the verandah,
the cat came out
tonight.

縁の下から猫が出て来た夜
En no shita kara neko ga dete kita yo

— HOSAI

Astonished,
the wild cat has caught
a skylark!

山猫のあつけとられし雲雀哉

Yamaneko no akke torareshi hibari kana

— ISSA

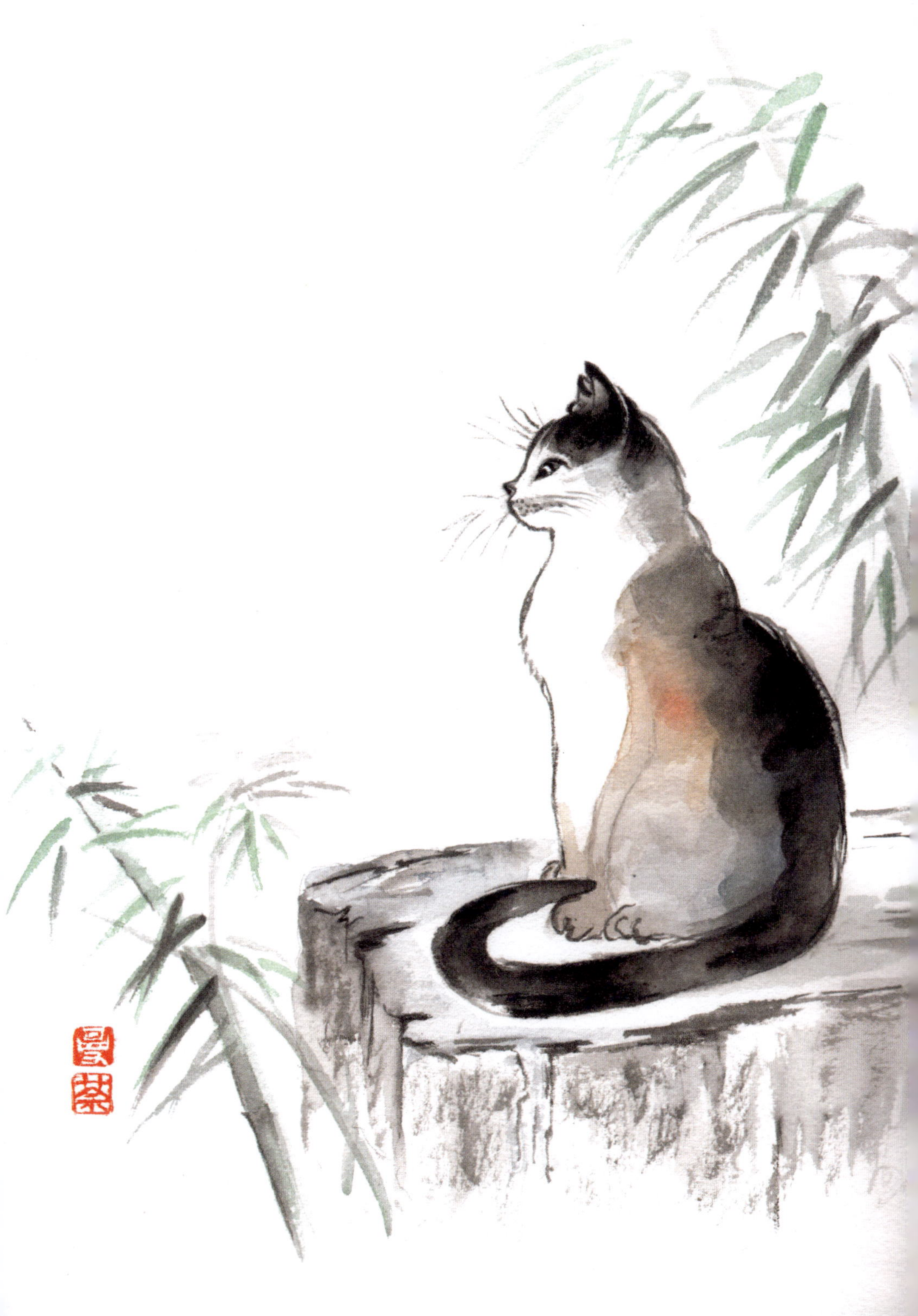

Shimmering air
rising lightly;
the cat's grave.

ちらちらと陽炎立ちぬ猫の塚
Chirachira to kagero tachinu neko no tsuka

— SOSEKI

Watching the cat
on the tub's lid,
the butterfly as it flies.

桶伏の猫を見舞ふやとぶ小蝶
Okebuse no neko wo mimau ya tobu kocho

— ISSA

The kitten
rubbing off fleas;
the nettle tree.

猫のこが蚤すりつける榎かな
Neko no ko ga nomi suritsukeru enoki kana

— ISSA

Is it from barley rice or love
she has grown thinner?
The cat's mate.

麦飯にやつるる恋か猫の妻
Mugi gohan ni yatsururu koi ka neko no tsuma

— BASHO

The large cat
hides its pee;
making flowers of snow.

大猫がしとかくす也花の雪
Oneko ga shito kakusu nari hana no yuki

— ISSA

Heavy dew;
crows call with the voices
of purring cats.

おく露や猫なで声の山鳥
Oku tsuyu ya neko nade koe no yamagarasu

— ISSA

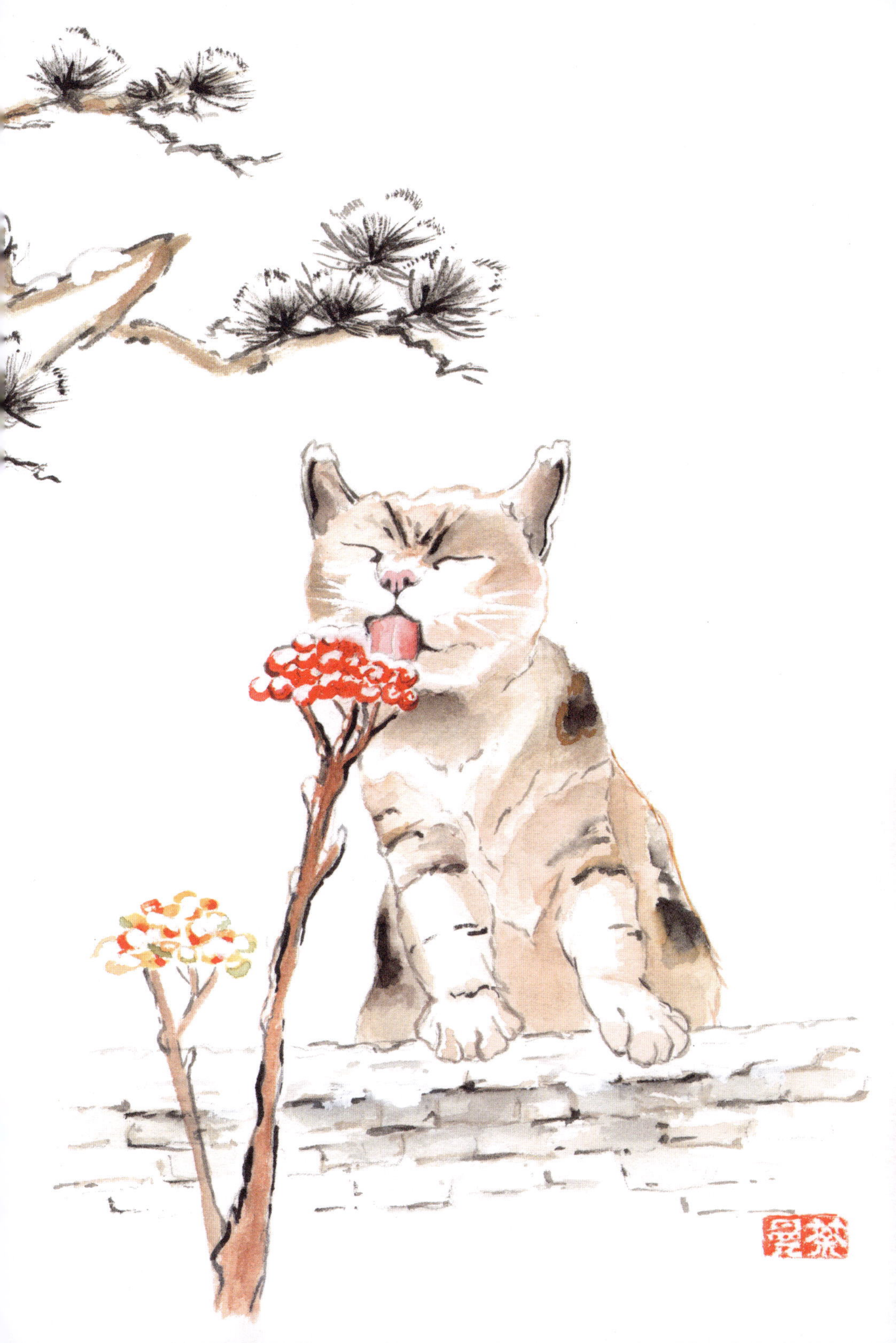

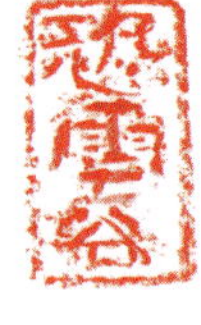

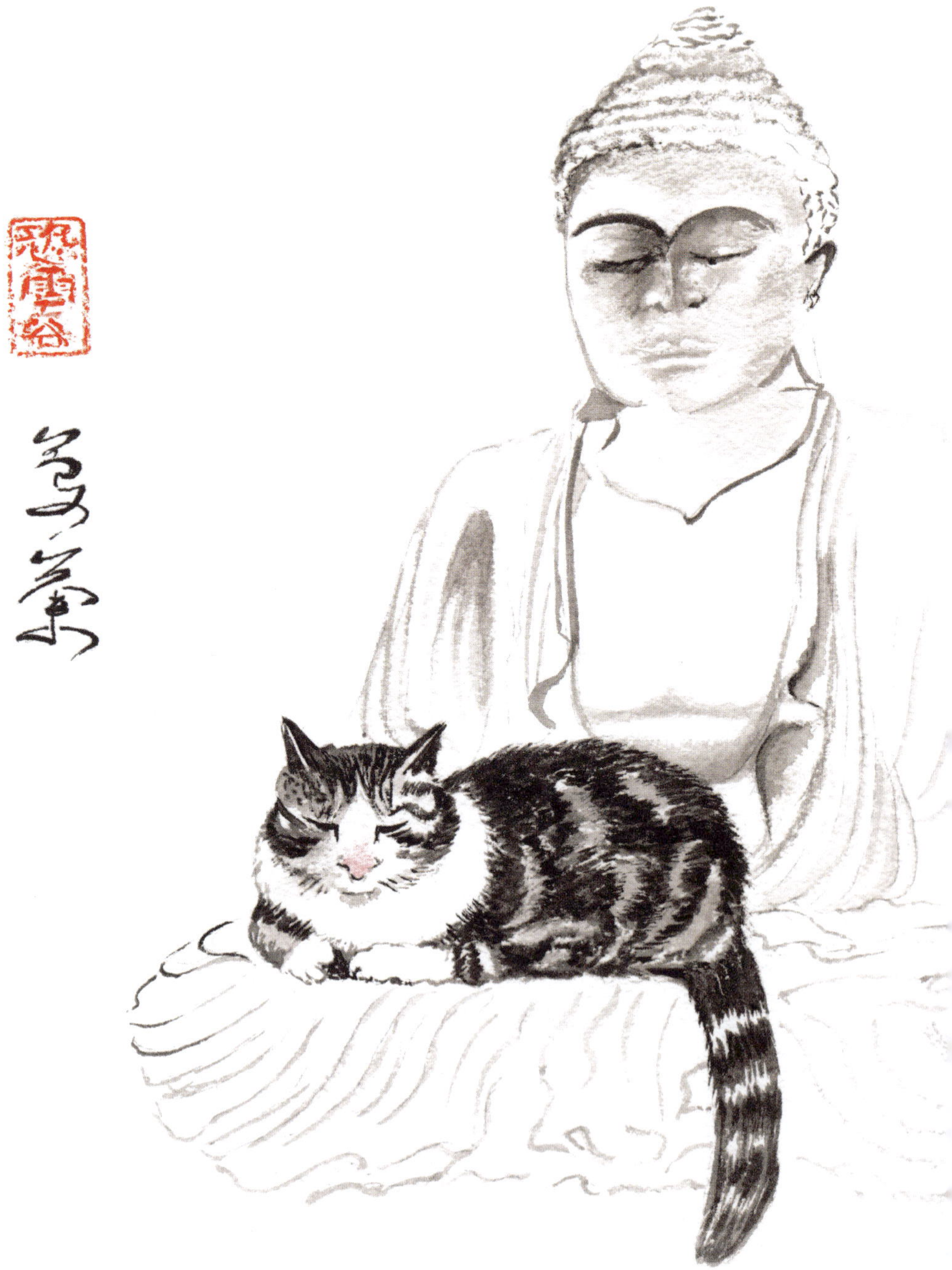

The stray cat
makes a pillow
of the Buddha's lap.

のら猫が仏のひざを枕哉
Nora neko ga hotoke no hiza wo makura kana

— ISSA

A house of bamboo grass,
a cat and the Buddha, too;
autumnal rains.

笹の家や猫も仏も秋の雨
Sasa no ie ya neko mo hotoke mo aki no ame

— ISSA

The fire watchman has not come again
to sound the alarm;
cats in love under the moon.

火の番またも鳴らし来ぬ恋猫の月
Hi no ban mata mo narashi konu koi neko no tsuki

— SANTOKA

Morning breeze;
around the mosquito netting
circles the cat.

朝風や蚊帳のまわりを廻る猫
Asa kaze ya kaya no mawari wo mawaru neko

— HASEGAWA

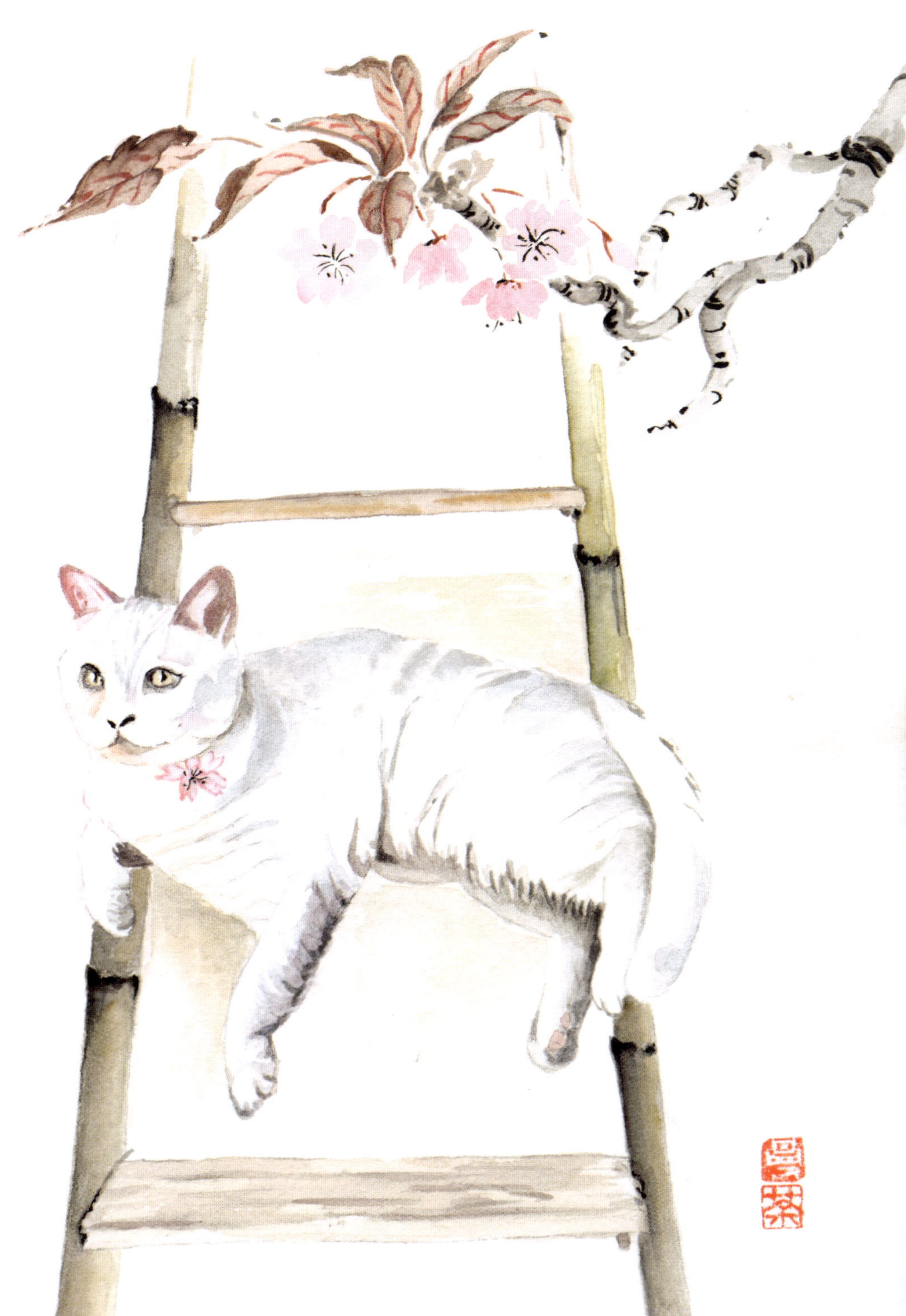

The cat's eyes
become needle thin;
the heat!

猫の目の針に成たる暑さかな
Neko no me no hari ni nasutaru atsusa kana

— SUIKO

Sleeping on the roof,
a cat with no master;
spring rain.

屋根寝主なし猫やの春雨
Yane nemuru shunashi neko ya no haru no ame

— TAIGI

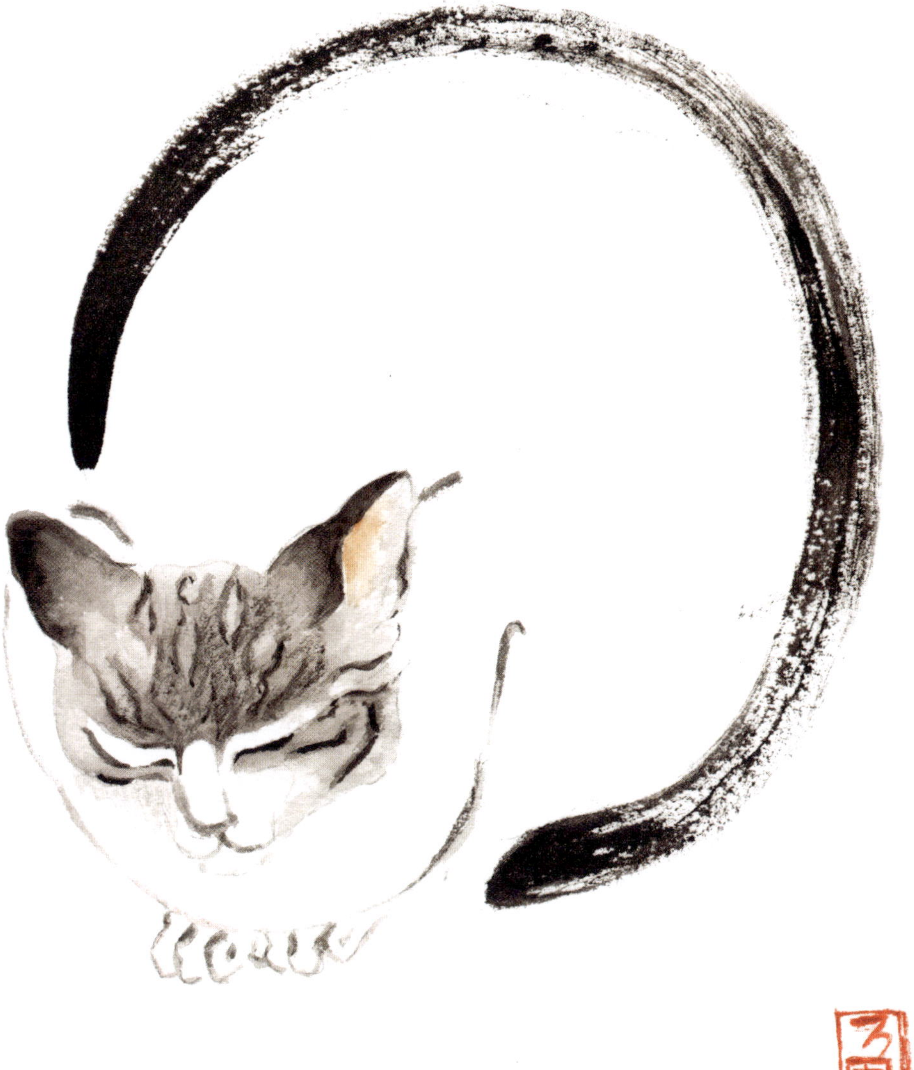

Chasing the chicken,
just having fun:
the tomcat.

うかれきて鶏追まくる男猫哉
Ukarekite tori oimakuru oneko kana

— ISSA

The cat's meal
shared
with a baby sparrow.

猫の飯相伴するや雀の子
Neko no meshi shoban suru ya suzume no ko

— ISSA

The cat scampers into the mulberry field.
A morning
of high wind.

猫がかけてはいる桑畑の風つのる朝
Neko ga kakete hairu kuwabatake no kaze tsunoru asa

— HEKIGODO

Just like a wife:
the cat's cry,
meow, meow.

妻こうやにょうにょうとなく猫の声
Tsuma ko ya nyo nyo to naku neko no koe

— SUTEJO

After I mopped it down,
the cat comes in
with muddy paws.

抜くあとから猫が泥足つけてくる

Nuku ato kara neko ga doroashi tsukete kuru

— HOSAI

Pushing through
four or five feet of snow:
cats in love.

四五尺の雪かき分けて猫の恋

Shigo shaku no yuki kakiwakete neko no koi

— ISSA

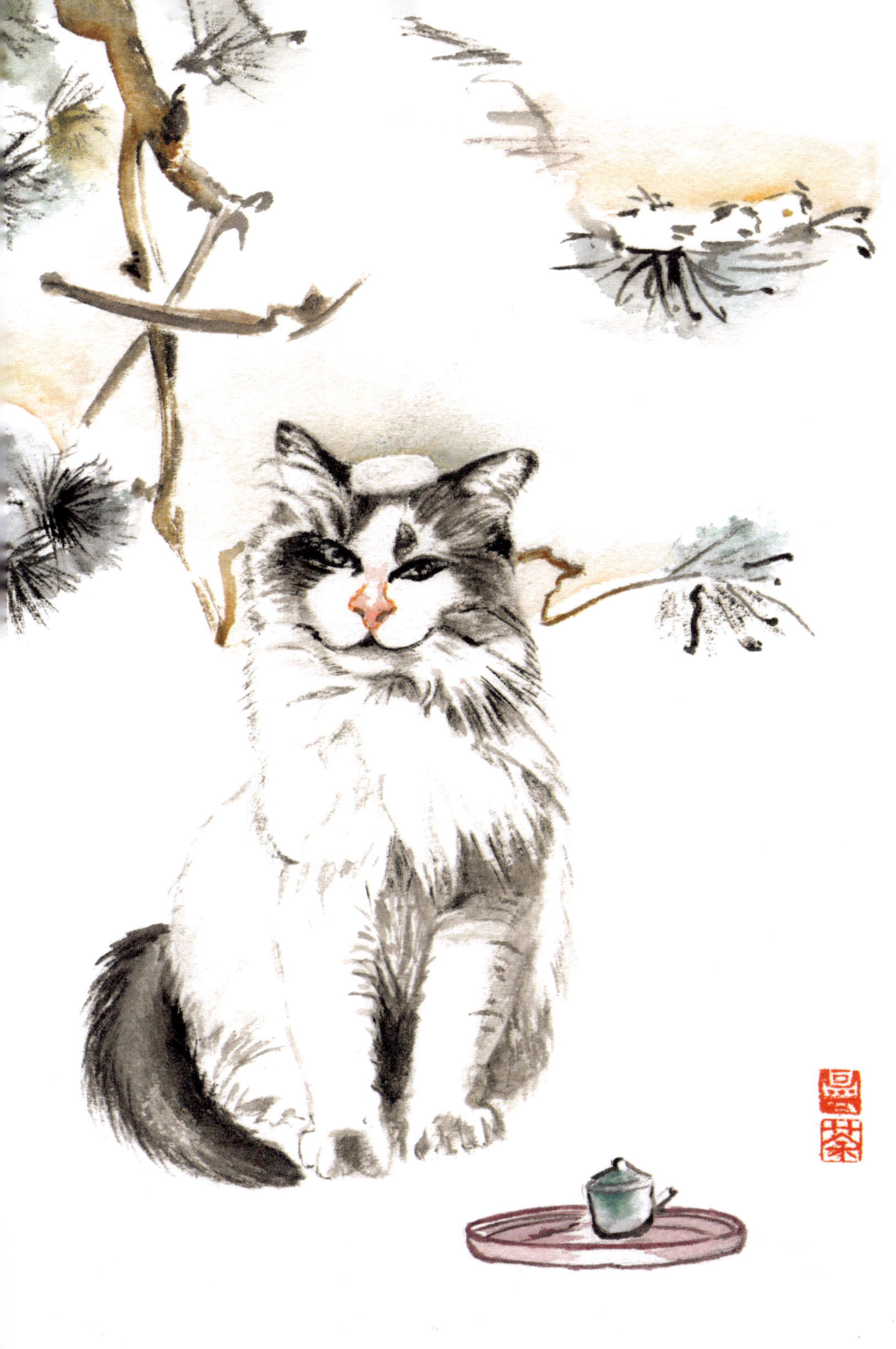

Batting
at the acorn:
the kitten.

団栗とはねっくらする子猫哉
Donguri to hanekkura suru koneko kana

— ISSA

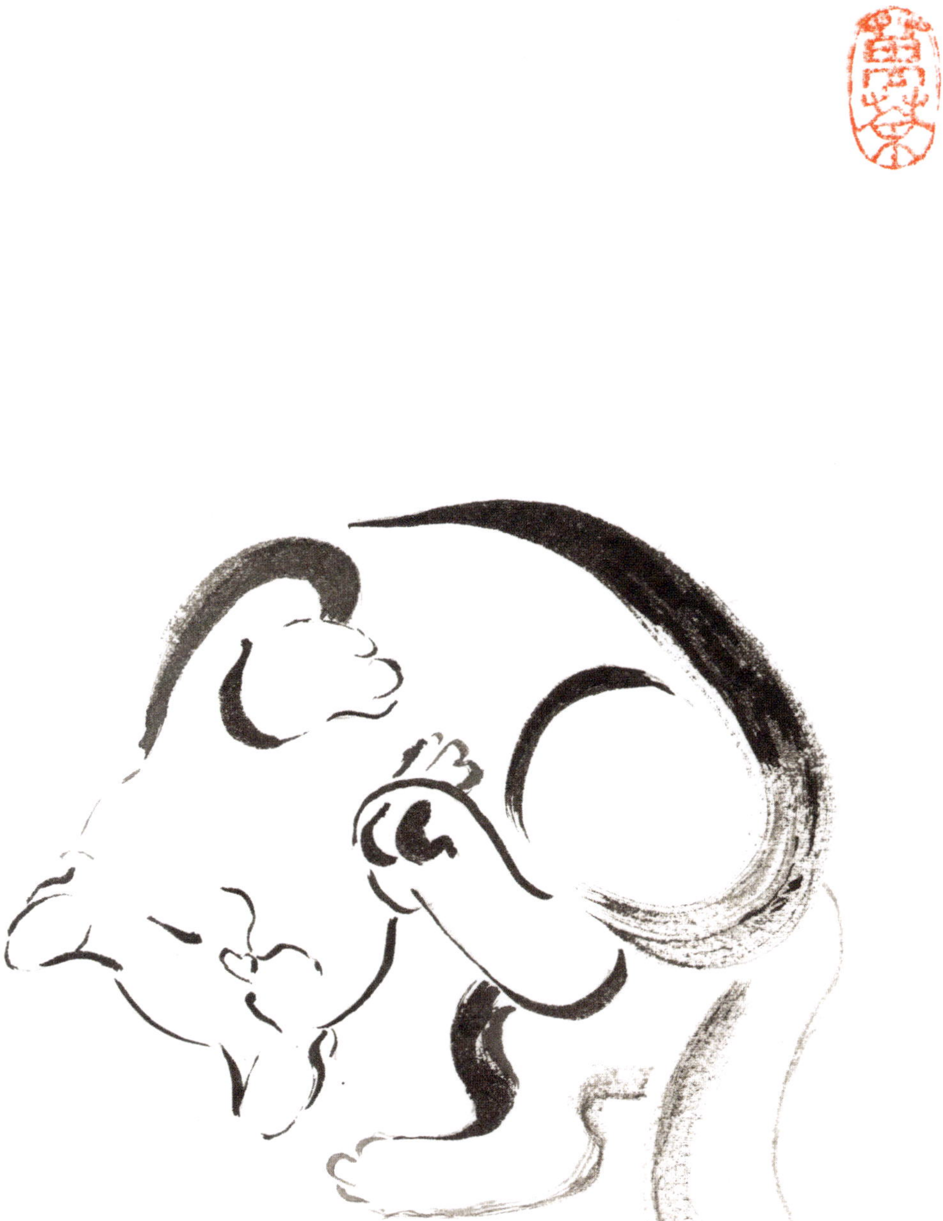

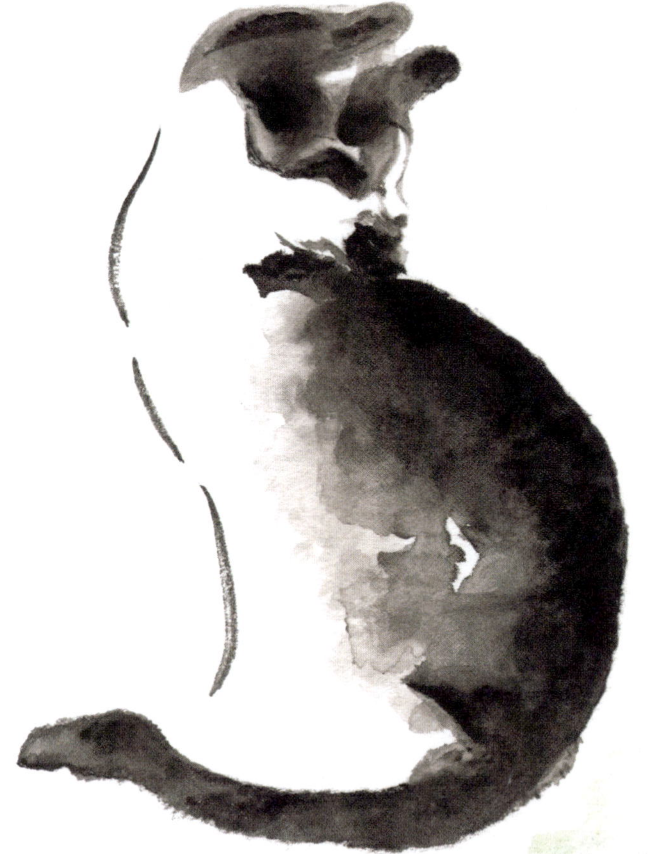
野筆
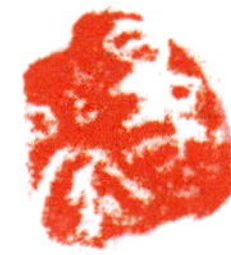

That insect!
Even while targeted by the cat,
it chirps.

あの虫や猫にねらはれながら鳴く
Ano mushi ya neko ni nerawarenagara naku

— ISSA

Eating up
the cat's meal:
the cricket.

猫の飯打ちくらひけりきりぎりす
Neko no meshi uchikuraikeri kirigirisu

— ISSA

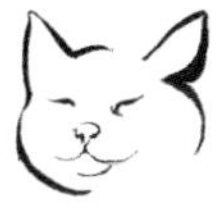

Biographies

Compiler and Illustrator

Thirty years ago, **Manda** felt the need to free herself from the constraints of the academy and decided to travel to Japan. Frequent stays there gave her the opportunity to adopt new practices. She learned from Japanese masters the "art of the line" as well as the mysteries of *haiga*, compositions where painted elements and poetry emerge from the same brush, forming a single entity. She has published many books, notably French translations of the works of Basho and Santoka. Her art appears in *The Illustrated Book of Japanese Haiku*, a collaboration with William Scott Wilson.

Translator

William Scott Wilson has published over twenty books including The Lone Samurai: *The Life of Miyamoto Musashi and The Life* and *Zen Haiku Poetry of Santoka Taneda*. His translation of the Hagakure, an 18th century treatise on samurai philosophy, was featured in the film *Ghost Dog* by the director Jim Jarmusch. Wilson was awarded a Commendation from the Foreign Ministry of Japan, and inducted into the Order of the Rising Sun by the Japanese emperor. He is also the author of *A Beginner's Guide to Japanese Haiku* and *The Illustrated Book of Japanese Haiku* (also in collaboration with Manda).

Published by Tuttle Publishing, an imprint of Periplus Editions (HK) Ltd.

www.tuttlepublishing.com

English translation © 2025 Periplus Editions (HK)

Illustrations © 2024 by Manda.
By arrangement with Synchronique Éditions sarl. Paris.

ISBN: 978-4-8053-2024-2

Library of Congress Cataloging-in Publication Data is in process.

Distributed by

North America, Latin America & Europe
Tuttle Publishing
364 Innovation Drive
North Clarendon
VT 05759-9436, USA
Tel: 1 (802) 773 8930; Fax: 1 (802) 773 6993
info@tuttlepublishing.com; www.tuttlepublishing.com

Japan
Tuttle Publishing
Yaekari Building 3rd Floor
5-4-12 Osaki
Shinagawa-ku
Tokyo 141-0032
Tel: (81) 3 5437-0171; Fax: (81) 3 5437-0755
sales@tuttle.co.jp; www.tuttle.co.jp

Asia Pacific
Berkeley Books Pte. Ltd.
3 Kallang Sector #04-01
Singapore 349278
Tel: (65) 67412178; Fax: (65) 67412179
inquiries@periplus.com.sg; www.tuttlepublishing.com

28 27 26 25   5 4 3 2 1
Printed in China   2509CM

GPSR Representative
Matt Parsons, matt.parsons@upi2mbooks.hr, UPI-2M PLUS d.o.o.,
Medulićeva 20, 10000, Zagreb, Croatia